WRITING LONG-RUNNING TELEVISION SERIES

WRITING LONG-RUNNING TELEVISION SERIES

Edited by Julian Friedmann and Pere Roca

With the collaboration of
Guy Meredith and Ruppert Widdicombe

Lectures from
the first PILOTS workshop

Sitges, Catalonia, Spain
June/October 1993

Written and presented by

Humphrey Barclay, Siegfried Braun, Jason Brett,
Lillie Ferrari, Rift Fournier, Julian Friedmann,
Jeanne Glynn, Adrian Hodges, Corinne Hollingworth,
Jeffrey Lewis, Caryn Mandabach, Guy Meredith,
Roberto Pace, Linda Seger, Stephan Warnik,
John Wells and Jürgen Wolf

MEDIA   A MEDIA BUSINESS SCHOOL PUBLICATION

© this collection FUNDACION CULTURAL MEDIA 1994

FIRST PUBLICATION 1994

© in each article is held by the author

ISBN 84-88773-02-1

Printed in Barcelona by Viking, SA. B-9.761 - 1994

Production coordinated by Hores extraordinàries

Designed by Víctor Oliva Pascuet

MEDIA BUSINESS SCHOOL
Torregalindo, 10-4º E-28016 Madrid
Phone 341/359 02 47 - 359 00 36 Fax 341/345 76 06

PILOTS
Diputació, 279-283, E-08007 Barcelona
Phone 343/488 10 38 Fax 343/487 41 92

CONTENTS

PARTNERS' FOREWORD

PILOTS is an initiative of the Media Business School in collaboration with the Generalitat de Catalunya and TV3, Televisió de Catalunya. It corresponds to the commitment of these three partners to contribute to improving television fiction in Europe.

The European audiovisual industry will improve if we are able to strengthen its two most solid pillars: cinema and television. PILOTS is proof of the firm desire of the three funding partners to work in both of these fields.

Furthermore, this collaboration is being carried out within the framework of an ever more frequent institutional arrangement: the collaboration of the Media Programme, through the MBS, with regional European governments and their television organisations.

Within the process of audiovisual production, the development and writing of scripts is, perhaps, the most fundamental element and the one that until now has had the least time and money devoted to it. The objective of PILOTS is to confront and solve this problem and, by publishing this book, to disseminate some basic arguments of the debate.

Fernando Labrada
Managing Director, MBS

Jaume Serrats
General Director of Cultural Promotion, Generalitat de Catalunya

Oleguer Sarsanedas
Programming Manager, Televisió de Catalunya

INTRODUCTION

The level of investment for a long-running series, even if it reaches a substantial audience in its country of origin, is nevertheless a major financial commitment for any broadcaster. Could PILOTS increase the audience both at home and in foreign markets?

The long-running series or serial is the foundation stone of the programme schedule for most networks in almost every country. The most internationally successful series and serials are usually written by teams of writers and script editors, a form of writing that differs not only from film and single plays, but also doesn't work to the same extent in Europe as it does in America and Australia, two countries particularly successful in exporting their long-running programmes.

PILOTS was devised to provide a focus and support system for writers and script editors in Europe, to take on the challenge of long-running series and serials, to increase the universal appeal of the projects, improving their chances of reaching wider audiences, while maintaining their specific cultural integrity.

Crossing borders does not mean coproductions. A current buzz-word in the industry is coproduction. Can money be found from multiple sources to help underwrite the costs of production? Co-finance seemed to us — as we began our first year — to be unlikely. Rather, we hoped to reduce the cost of the programme, not by cutting the budget, but by reaching bigger audiences.

It is our belief that one of the best ways of achieving this is to establish the importance of the script editor as a key member of the creative team, something that is not common in most European countries. Script editing is not often seen as a discipline for which you can train. Script editors in Europe are not paid as well as they are across the Atlantic nor are they accorded anything like the respect they should be.

The book which we are now publishing is the first step towards expanding the services which PILOTS offers beyond the intensive workshops in which participants take part.

Of course, by simply reading this book you cannot acquire more than a minimal idea of what really happened during the workshops. It doesn't provide a ringside seat for the animated debates on the participating scripts, nor does it convey the enthusiastic participation in the collective exercises run by the specialists, and it can't give you a personal introduction to the Head of Programmes or Head of Drama whom you are unlikely to meet at that International Market; nor can the reader benefit from the interaction generated by ten television projects all being written at the same time and in the same place. But reading this book does open a door to all these things and for many it might be the first step towards creating a common ground for reflection.

The long-running fiction series has not had very much written about it and even less professional acknowledgement. The European attitude towards television series has tended to be, apart from a few glorious exceptions, somewhat neglectful: Americans and others took the initiative. When it WAS up to us to write series, we treated them as a minor genre to which the least possible time and money was allocated.

The lectures given by our tutors, godparents and specialists during the PILOTS 93 workshops form the basic core of this publication. They have been divided into two groups — those which have been transcribed and those we have only been able to summarise or mention briefly. The reason for this choice is in no way one of quality, but of pragmatism. Many of the things which were said during the workshops were directly related to the participating projects or to some activity of the programme — screenings, round tables, or seminars. It was difficult to reproduce some of these contributions out of context, and they have therefore been omitted or only summarised.

We trust that the publication of this book will contribute towards our goal of pushing European drama series into new markets — both domestic and foreign. PILOTS, despite its limited structure, should represent much more than just the celebration of its workshops. We hope this book will become a point of reference for all those who are interested in improving the development and writing of European television series.

It is the intention of future PILOTS workshops, set in the charming Catalan seaside town of Sitges, to develop powerful and creative writing teams, who will produce the most appreciated and successful TV series in Europe in the next few years. Judging by the generosity of our hosts and sponsors, the inspiration of our tutors and specialists, the dedication of our staff and the enthusiasm of the participants, this should be attainable.

But all this would never have been possible without the inspiration and the support of: Holde Lhoest, Head of the MEDIA Programme; Gudie Lawaetz, former General Manager of the MBS; Fernando Labrada, General Manager of the MBS; Antonio Saura, Nadine Luque and Isabel de las Casas, of the MBS; Antoni Kirchner, of the Generalitat de Catalunya; Oleguer Sarsanedas and Josep Lluís Comerón, of Televisió de Catalunya; and Thomas Spieker, as consultant to the Generalitat de Catalunya. Finally, special thanks to Jane Busfield, Judi Sydes, Heather Wylie and Inés Roca.

Julian Friedmann
Head of Studies

Pere Roca
Managing Director

THE DESCRIPTION OF PILOTS

The objective of PILOTS is to improve the quality of long-running series produced in Europe, raising the standards of script writing and increasing the ability of European series to reach larger audiences and "cross borders".

PILOTS is a non-profit making, autonomous association, led by a General Council and an Executive Committee whose members have been appointed by the partners of the programme: Media Business School (a MEDIA Programme), Generalitat de Catalunya and Televisió de Catalunya.

PARTICIPANTS

Broadcasters and independent producers with a long-running series project and a writing team, from European Union and EFTA member states. The teams consist of script editors and producers, and one or more writers. Great emphasis is placed on the role of the script editor.

THE WORKSHOPS

The teams work together with PILOTS for a period of five months. This encompasses two residential workshops with a period between them. The programme employs three learning techniques.

- The first is didactic: lectures, seminars, analyses of drama series episodes. Experts lead these sessions which also involve interaction among the participants.

- The second technique requires all the participants to read, analyse and criticise each other's work. Through this method, the participants learn how to accept constructive criticism, and about the needs and the expectations of audiences in other countries.

- The third technique involves the actual rewriting of their pilot scripts and bibles by participants, under close supervision from the tutors.

The First Workshop

At the start, each team presents its project to the attending experts and to the other teams. Subsequently, lectures on a range of subjects are given by specialists, while technical writing and editing skills are developed, under the guidance of experts. Each team has its bible analysed and all participants have the opportunity of discussing their projects at length with tutors, godparents and specialists.

At the end of the workshop, the teams receive specific instructions for rewriting their bible and script on returning to their countries.

Between the Workshops

During the three month period between the workshops, each team rewrites its script and writes another episode. These are read by tutors and godparents, who are available for consultation by the participants. Notes are provided to the teams for further rewrites, where necessary. Tutors will meet with the teams in the team's country for a two day session.

The Second Workshop

Each day there is a lecture, given by a guest specialist, tutor or godparent, followed by a discussion. Afternoon sessions might start with a round-table discussion, seminars on particular subjects or a screening, but are largely devoted to rewriting. In the evening, episodes related to the following day's lecture are screened on the hotel video channel.

THE EXPERTS

Tutors

The tutors have a supervisory role. They are experienced writers or script editors and they attend both workshops.

Godparents

The godparent assesses the viability of the project in the market as well as its commercial potential. Godparents are senior broadcasting executives with long-running series experience.

Specialists

The specialists include story analysts, writers, script editors and producers, from the USA, Europe and Australia.

FURTHER INFORMATION

PILOTS is based in Catalonia, with an office in Barcelona and training facilities for its workshops in Sitges, a coastal village 20 km. south of the city. The Participation Fee is 20.000 ECU per team of three people. This covers all travel, hotels, meals and the organisational and administrative costs of the programme. In addition, participants have access to all site facilities, including use of word processors, video equipment, a specialised library of books, articles, videos and scripts, in the Palau Maricel, the restored museum building in which the workshops take place.

SITGES: THE AFTERWORD

GUY MEREDITH

We were sitting in front of the hotel, a dozen of us, on a sunlit November afternoon, waiting for the minibus to the airport, gazing at the waves. In a simple yet touching ceremony earlier, the volleyball had been punted blindly out to sea from the terrace of the Maricel; no-one had sung karaoke for hours. Brian said, "You know one really good thing? You get all these writers together for all this time and nobody says what writers always say to each other, in that bitchy way: 'So what are *you* working on?'"

"That's right," I nodded, noticing from this angle that there was a row of houses between the Maricel and the sea and that even now some local resident might be the proud possessor of a nearly-new volleyball and a broken window.

"So what are *you* working on?" said Brian, just for the hell of it.

"Can't remember. You?"

It's really dangerous, actually, taking a bunch of writers out of their half-lit garrets and plonking them in a four-star, seafront hotel. Implying that they've got to socialise, keep regular hours, eat with a knife and fork. The producers of course were in their element, snapping for service with fingers whose prints had long since been worn smooth. But the scribes — some of us had been writing for decades, God knows, we were the next thing to troglodytes! Makes you wonder how they sold the deal to the hotel. Probably softened them up by telling them they were getting a large rock group.

No doubt the atmosphere of the Palau Maricel helped. You climbed the stone steps, you walked through the main doors into what served as the lecture hall and suddenly a feeling of almost religious awe overcame you. The more perceptive participants put this down to the ten foot statue of the Virgin Mary that looked down from a side chapel. Others, maybe just less sold on iconography, might have felt that here was somewhere you would be changed by, converted, that your lives would be kinked for the first time since that wild decision not to become a dentist all those years ago.

And in truth, there was wisdom. And in wisdom, truth. From the platform, speakers from America and Europe gave the benefit of their experience, some with film clips, some with graphs, some with left side of the brain exercises. At the very least, whether writer or producer, you saw how others had suffered for their projects and lived to tell the tale. From the Americans particularly a feeling of optimism emanated, that if you believed hard enough in what you were doing, if you rewrote it and rewrote it and *rewrote* it, it would eventually see the screen. European speakers, particularly those corralled into speculating on broadcasting trends, were more cautious. 'Let's hope we've still got an industry in ten years' time was the rumbling bass motif. Well, that was what we were there to help try and ensure, wasn't it?

Long-running series, whether drama or sitcom, are a battleground, without a doubt. They are where audience loyalty can be established or snatched from a rival channel. They are where national tastes can be both satisfied and entrenched. All you have to do is convince your audience that your series is better than anything that can be brought in from across the Atlantic. And the Americans, bless them, were there to help us do that.

From expounding the complications of team writing to detailed analyses of hit comedy shows, the idea of the talks was to provoke fresh insights into the process of creating television. Maybe there was no experience on hand that couldn't have been gleaned from books, maybe even from sitting around long enough and thinking of new ways to go about things. But even being in the same room as someone who'd made a lot of money writing "**Hill Street Blues**" (yes, made a lot of money *writing*) induced a sort of wilful osmosis. You wanted to sit down then and there and create your TV masterpiece. Which was precisely the opportunity that PILOTS was designed to give you.

But of course nothing's that easy. There are always obstacles. For instance, after a morning of lecture and discussion, suddenly you'd bump into the Spanish timetable. The Spanish timetable sits up and says, "Hey, it's lunch. It's warm. Come up on the terrace, eat your way through three courses and have a little wine while you're at it." What the Spanish timetable does after that is go for a siesta. What the PILOTS participant did, at least in the beginning, was go straight back for another lecture. Anyone who took the platform p.m. was faced with the sight of fifty people all trying to sit behind each other. Something had to give. Lunch was extended.

> " *Long-running series, whether drama or sitcom, are a battleground, without a doubt. They are where audience loyalty can be established or snatched from a rival channel.* "

The real integration, however, came in the evening, when each participant became the owner of a meal voucher worth 2,000 pesetas and a numbered list of restaurants which would accept such currency. The streets filled with national groups scrutinising maps like tank commanders before a campaign: "Number 2? Where is number 2?", "If we go through there I'm sure we come in at the *back* of number 16" And with the Icelanders the only nationality catered for by a tailor-made establishment, "Los Vikingos", (the Germans searched in vain for "Los Visigoths" — no Sitges restauranteur had seen it as a crowd puller) it wasn't long before paths were crossing and the international language of food ("Number 8? Yes, number 8 is down here!") was weaving its magic charms.

So what of the projects? Wasn't there a Superproject here, something we could all work on, an Arianne of the airwaves? After all, we were only five nations and if the British could fit in without rubbing everyone up the wrong way (well, they had already imposed English on the whole venture and so could presumably afford a bit of give and take) surely there was room for international co-operation? Early discussions took place and log-lines whistled through the air like arrow shafts ("Just when you thought it was safe to go back in the water, the beach was far too crowded with a fascinating, cosmopolitan mix of...", "In the European Parliament, everyone can hear you scream", "Jeremy Irons *is* Juan Gonzalez, an Icelandic taxi driver working in Hamburg, who one day, after inadvertently crossing the Danish border..."). But in the end, ever-alert to the smouldering dangers of Europudding, the participants returned to their own narrow, national interests and were to be found like Conradian conspirators, huddled in the far corners of the Palau Maricel, plotting their own project's advancement.

Which was where we left it, at the end of June, for a theoretical summer of hard work. On reconvening in October there was a certain amount of initial bluster about leaps of progress but it was soon clear that, by and large, leisure had taken its toll. But when the Head of Studies weighed in on day two with a lecture on how to pitch your project in one minute, which was only a preface to facing real broadcasters, it was clear we were into Workshop II: This Time It's Personal. Teams soon shaped up again to decide what their project was *really* about.

Once past the trauma of the pitching sessions — in which teams were filmed being nervous in front of a panel of stern-faced inquisitors and the results shown on the hotel's video channel, much to the perplexity no doubt of the non-PILOTS guests who probably felt they'd stumbled upon some minimalist art movie — the last week of the programme hove into view. And the fact that projects were now making advances in terms of words on discs became apparent. Suddenly, fewer writers were struggling the 200 metres from the hotel to the Palau of a morning, and this despite the fact that the summer conviviality of Sitges had dispersed with the tourists and you could stroll from one end to the other of the town's Sin Street in two minutes and without even a sniff of veniality.

Yes, the urgency of autumn was upon us and deadlines fixed in the carefree youth of spring were approaching. Now had the lessons of the lectures to be applied, now the sly art of the tutors consulted, the wheat of the scripts winnowed from the chaff. If Virgil had been among us, many a hexameter would have sprung to his lips to describe the industry with which portable computers were being pummelled. Though of course he would have had to address remarks through the chairman and wait for the microphone before declaiming.

It was at this stage, with writers returning to their normal reclusive selves and those producers still present reduced to the hapless role of urging them on, that PILOTS' two trump cards — not even in the pack when the workshops began — were produced. A beach emptied of holidaymakers is freed up for sporting activity. And in a deserted seaside resort, no-one can hear you sing. Art and recreation, volleyball and karaoke, lunchtime and evening — the twin columns around which the communal spirit of PILOTS was reconstructed.

Because as much as anything else, the inspiration which PILOTS gave to its participants came from living amongst a microcosm of the Continent's television industry, from feeling that others are facing the same problems. Few sessions were as lively, or indeed as informative, as those in which living scripts — by non-participants — were torn limb from limb; from criticising the work of others it's only a short step to casting a jaundiced eye over your own and then you're back on the rewriting road indicated by so many of the lecturers. No-one who attended the workshops, whether participant, tutor or even specialist, seemed to come away feeling their time had been less than well spent; lessons *had* been learned, contacts made and most of the projects immeasurably improved.

Were there drawbacks? Yes, without a doubt. Barcelona is tantalisingly close but you're lucky if you get to see it, except on a communal outing. In fact, the timetable is so intense that most of Sitges, beautiful as it is between the hills and the water, remains foreign territory during daylight. As for writing, it's only in films that a hotel bedroom provides the ideal surroundings; despite other amenities, the lack of soundproofing (in the Hotel San Sebastian Playa, everyone can hear you whisper) meant that concentration levels needed to be particularly high. And with broadcasters around an edginess set in when projects still in the tender stages of development had to be exposed to the light of day.

But that's life. Writers, as part of their chosen vocation, are closeted away from the world most of the time. Their nearest contact with the rest of the planet might be through the producer (only half way to being a member of the human race) and that only as an occasional phone call. In Sitges they were thrown into the triple maelstrom of education, communication *and* creation, not to mention seeing their producer on a daily basis. It was worthwhile but it was tough. No wonder they didn't have the energy left to bitch about each other.

LECTURES

DEVELOPMENT HELL: THE PROCESS OF CREATING TV IN THE US

JASON BRETT

Jason Brett is currently creating, developing, writing and producing series for TriStar Television, and is also producing Jim Belushi's latest feature film. His background includes writing and producing for motion pictures as well as for all the US networks.

I'm going to talk about the process of creating and developing television in the US — a process which I call 'development hell' for reasons which should become clearer as we go along.

I knew very little about the European method of developing television prior to coming here, but I can tell you already that there is one striking similarity. When you want to develop a show, you petition a government agency, and when *I* want to develop a show, I petition a network. But once a project's accepted, the government leaves you alone. I have to deal with the smothering love of a network. By way of an explanation, I am what is referred to in my industry as writer-producer and show-runner. That means that I create my own shows and run the series once they go into production. When I write a pilot script I'm paid by a production company which is reimbursed by a network. Production companies 'umbrella' projects in the US, which means that for agreeing to advance all the upfront and development costs and make up the difference between what it costs to make the show and what the network pays to licence that show, they basically beat out my share of the back-end profits, if any — which statistically speaking, as you can imagine, happens very rarely.

So, I come up with a project and take it to a production company and we agree to partner. Now we go to the network together to pitch the project, which is typically done during something called the "pitch season".

We should talk about that phenomenon for a minute: a pitch is the act of presenting your idea to the network. It's one part substance to two parts performance, and no matter how good your idea is, there's a whole art to pitching. The fact is that if you want to be a good television producer in the US it helps to be a good entertainer, and believe me, there's no tougher room than a room full of suits. It's like telling your story to an oil painting. The pitch season as it's called is something akin to the mating season, an annual ritual when writers, producers, actors and production companies all trot *en masse* into the networks to present their ideas over a three to four month period, from July to November.

> " A pitch is the act of presenting your idea to the network. It's one part substance to two parts performance. "

Let me put this process into some perspective for you. There are four major television networks in the US — I'm talking about commercial television — NBC, ABC, CBS and FBN (Fox Broadcasting Network). They each have at least two development executives who, during the so-called "pitch season", will often be subjected to several pitches a day, for several days a week, over a period of several months. In broad numbers, we're talking about hundreds of ideas presented to the networks each year.

Today, a network may develop as few as thirty-five projects from the hundreds they hear, meaning a writer-producer has — walking in the door — less than a 20% chance of his/her idea being bought by a network and developed into a script. Of those projects that are bought and go to script, a network is likely to go to pilot on less than half of them, and of those pilots produced, less than half of *those* will get a series order. So as you can see, the chance of a pitched idea making it all the way through the development process and onto the network schedule as a series is extremely slight. Add to this equation the limited number of series that last more than three seasons, and you begin to get the idea what "development hell" really is.

The American system is a factory, and as in any factory there's a large degree of waste and inefficiency. Just look at how much money is being thrown away just to find a dozen new shows to air every year. But every industry needs some form of research and development, and when the television industry works it works very well. Don't get me wrong: it works in spite of the intrusive and bubble-headed interference of the networks. Nevertheless, each pitch season does yield at least one hit show.

When I started writing for television, I didn't know much about the medium but I had the opportunity to work with some wonderfully talented mentors, and from them I learnt that there's a certain kind of formula for sitcom and a certain kind for one-hour drama. But the big question is, is there a formula for successful television? And I'm going to tell you, from my experience in television, the answer is unequivocally … maybe! As I talk about the development process today, I will mention many successful shows which I believe exemplify the qualities inherent in most of the successful long-running series, and by the end we'll see if there's a formula. But before that I'm going to give you a hint. In thinking about it and talking to several of my colleagues before coming here, I can say there are definitely four basic components that can be identified with the success of every sucessful long-running television series. So let's talk about development by starting where we all begin, as writers, which is with CONCEPT.

CONCEPT

The concept is the basic premise of a show. A single father takes a job as a live-in domestic for a working mother. Or a writer of mystery novels uses her craft to solve murders. A scientist is exposed to radiation and mutates into a green monster every time he experiences rage. Concepts come from anywhere. I draw my inspiration from characters or a situation. What I always do when I come up with an idea is ask myself three basic questions. Is it a television idea rather than a film idea? Is it produceable on a weekly basis and is it sustainable over time? Television, and particularly commmerical television, is a very distinctive medium with its own qualities and constraints. It's one thing to want to do a series about the first colony on Mars, but it's a different thing to produce it and sustain it on a week to week basis. It is important that we as writers understand the medium we are working in so we don't frustate ourselves working in opposition to it.

So I'm thinking about my concept. Television executives will tell you that shows with strong concepts cross borders better and are typically more successful internationally. "**Robocop**" and "**The New Adventures of Superman**" are two series based on traditional action heroes which haven't even started production yet and are already generating huge worldwide sales. These shows are what television executives call 'high concept', which essentially means that the premise of the show can be simply communicated in a single phrase or sentence.

> " *What I always do when I come up with an idea is ask myself three basic questions. Is it a television idea rather than a film idea? Is it produceable on a weekly basis and is it sustainable over time?* "

Concept is defined by three essential elements, starting with the most essential element of all: CHARACTER. The key to creating successful TV lies in creating a character whom your audience wants to watch, then having your character live up to your audience's expectations week after week. Really good TV shows are about character interaction and relationships, and once we invent our characters, concept effectively ceases to be important. It's when we create our characters that our projects come to life.

A good TV show has characters whom we feel we know, people we recognise, who act and behave as we would. When we look at them we see ourselves or family members or people we work with. We almost expect to see them at a market, or standing in line at a movie theatre. They have lives, emotions, points of view. And like people in real life, they seem three-dimensional because they have conflicts and flaws. "**I**

Love Lucy", "The Honeymooners", "MASH", "All in the Family", classic character-driven comedies that seem timeless because their characters are so well observed. They're funny not because the characters say funny things, but because we know the characters saying the line so well. Why do shows as old as "**Dallas**" or "**Columbo**" still hold up, where "**Miami Vice**", for example, doesn't? Characters.

In sitcom the characters are typically an ensemble of odd eccentrics and stock characters straight out of *commedia dell'arte*. Look, for instance, at "**The Mary Tyler Moore Show**". Lou Grant, the crusty but lovable boss; Ted, the buffoonish co-worker; Murray the confidante; Betty the saucy bitch. It's Moliere. Or "**Cheers**": you've got Sam Malone, the sex maniac; Carla the wise-arse; Woodie the dumb co-worker; Norm the fat guy; Frasier the fop. Notice the constrast. There's a vivid range between these characters. It's really clean. Successful American sitcoms don't try to change the conventions of the genre. They adhere to cast structure and character prototype, but then distinguish themselves in the exploration of those characters through stories. With sitcom the plots are just vehicles to allow the characters to be vengeful, vexed, perplexed, conniving, goofy, or whatever it is that those characters do best.

> " *Whether your show is a one-hour or a half-hour, try to limit your characters, and pick a central character or character relationship, a point of view, through which the show speaks.* "

Whether your show is a one-hour or a half-hour, try to limit your characters, and pick a central character or character relationship, a point of view, through which the show speaks. Find the voice in your show, and that voice is either a character or a character relationship. Too often we, as writers, define our characters by occupation and forget to add the idiosyncracies which make them lifelike. Take your detective and make him a fumbling, mumbling distracted guy in a rumpled raincoat and what have you got? You've got Columbo. Take a local TV news producer and make her naive and lovable and so achingly fragile that you're afraid she'll break and what have you got? You've got Mary Richards in "**The Mary Tyler Moore Show**". Take a bluecollar bus driver and make him bombastic and bigger than life, a man as king of his castle, an old-fashioned kind of guy, and what have you got? You've got Ralph Kramden of "**The Honeymooners**".

To breathe life into a character a writer must go way beyond the basics of their race, their sex, their ethnicity, their physical attributes, their background, their life-styles, all that stuff that we necessarily do initially to blueprint our characters. In fact, the line between fact and fantasy can blur so much at times that it can really confuse people. You might have heard about our former vice-president's outrage last year over Murphy Brown's decision to have a child out of wedlock. Now that's how real Murphy Brown was to Dan Quayle. A lot of Americans wished he was a fictitious character!

THEME

So once we've got our character we need to define what our show's about. Which is THEME. Theme is the compass which steers the show. Successful long-running TV series typically have strong themes. In fact a strong theme can often elevate a mediocre premise into something really worthwhile. Ken Johnson, a writer-producer who started his career writing the science-fiction action series "**The Bionic Man**", took a dopey, comic-book premise about a scientist who turns into a green monster every time he gets mad, and transformed it into "**The Incredible Hulk**". He applied a theme, the rage within man, and the show became about man trying to control his internal rage. He explored the causes of rage, he explained it, sometimes even justified it. With a compelling theme, the show took something monstrous and humanised it. And because of that, this gimmicky comic-book action show was able to tackle some real social issues. Don't get me wrong. I'm not holding up "**The Incredible Hulk**" as the pinnacle of achievement, but I do think it has merit, particularly in the context of talking about theme.

The other thing to bear in mind is that theme crosses borders, it's a common language. Every culture can relate to such universal themes as the division of the classes, which is "**Roseanne**", or the competitiveness among men which is "**Home Improvement**", or the corrupting influence of money which is "**Dallas**", or the outrage of war which is "**MASH**". Universal themes truly cross borders.

Themes give a show a touchstone to return to week after week, a vision. And successful TV shows are shows where absolutely everyone involved, from creators, writers and directors through to the props department, throroughly understands the show they're doing and what it's about. The job of anyone creating a new show is to know what the show's about and to define it in terms of the theme. Later on, once the show's up and running, the writing staff will thank you for that, because character plus theme equals stories.

TONE

Once I've got my characters and theme, I start thinking in terms of attitude. And that brings me to TONE. Tone declares your creative point of view about your idea. Take the dark concept of a wartime medical unit and add an ironic tone and you've got "MASH". Lay melodrama over the story of a backstabbing Texas oil family and you've got "Dallas". Mix social satire into the adventures of a dysfunctional cartoon family and you've got "The Simpsons". Tone informs every creative decision. It's like a colour-scheme matrix that I lay over my show to define my point of view about my characters, their lives and their stories. It determines everything from the dialogue to the pace to the plot.

> " I've got my CONCEPT, I've got my CHARACTERS, I've got the THEME and the TONE, so now I know exactly what my show is. "

Tone even determines the best setting for a show, which in turn determines the best format for a show, whether its a half-hour comedy set in the workplace or a one-hour drama set on the streets of LA or a whimsical half-hour set in suburban America during the '60s like "The Wonder Years", or an hour's satire set in modern Alaska like "Northern Exposure". Tone tells me whether a show should be videotaped, filmed in front of an audience on set or shot on location. Tone is the last, but by no means the least, of the defining elements of concept, the first component of successful long-running TV series.

I've got my CONCEPT, I've got my CHARACTERS, I've got the THEME and the TONE, so now I know exactly what my show is. So I drop myself into a production company, we agree to partner, and off we go to the network to pitch my project. The network loves the idea and I, the writer, now go off to write the pilot script. As we all know, the pilot script's a prototype, the writer's equivalent to industry's proof of concept. There are 2 types of pilot: the premise pilot or something called the sample episode. Premise pilots establish the characters, concept and theme as well as inform the back story and point the direction in which the show's going to go. A sample episode pilot assumes the show's already in its first season so it's written just like a typical episode, with the characters and relationships already well-established.

For purposes of moving on, let's just say that I wrote a brilliant pilot, the network loved it and they have put my series on the air and now it's a huge hit and it's pulling huge numbers. What's the second component of a successful long-running TV series?

EXECUTION

Did you ever hear the expression, "careful what you wish for, it might happen"? Well, 'development hell' seems easy compared to the next phase: 'production hell, the nightmare continues'. If you're one of the statistical few who end up with a show on the network schedule, say goodbye to the rest of your life for a while. For a show to become a successful long-running series, every aspect of the production machinery has to work at peak performance to crank out shows that meet the same exacting standards week after week after week. This is where the writer-producer makes the transition into something we call a show-runner. Show-runners make obscene amounts of money. It takes a combination of creative talent, and sheer nuts-and-bolts experience, and it starts with vision — the ability to project a show into its future, to know how to evolve it and where to take each individual character and how to keep the audience interested and committed. A show-runner arcs a season's worth of shows like a writer structures a script. With a season opener, a beginning, a first-act ending, which is your holiday show that in America would either be a Thanksgiving or a Christmas show; a mid-point two-parter which comes during something called 'sweeps week', which is where the advertising agencies set their rates on the basis of the popularity of a show, so you're going to do a really high-concept show during sweeps week; and a season's closer, which is an intriguing development to make sure the audience returns to the show in the fall.

Like everything else in this process, there's a craft to doing this, a fine line which, if you cross it, you take your characters too far afield and you risk losing your audience. And what kept "**Cheers**", "**The Cosby Show**" and "**MASH**" in the top ten for so many years? Writing. Writing is the bread and butter of successful TV. As the character is the key to creating a successful show, writing is the key to sustaining it. And not just good writing: *great* writing and endless, ENDLESS REWRITING. There's a saying that goes, "If it ain't on the page, it ain't on the stage". It takes craft to crank out good scripts week after week. If the script isn't playing, if the dialogue is flat, if there's a problem with the structure of the show, it's the show-runner's job to fix it in time to make the schedule. Regardless of how big the show's writing staff might be, most show-runners take the final pass on each and every script to make sure each show has a singular voice.

> " *What kept "Cheers", "Cosby" and "MASH" in the top ten for so many years? Writing. Writing is the bread and butter of successful TV.* "

What else is necessary to execute a show and to keep it on its feet? STORIES. Remember what I said earlier, character plus theme equals stories. If the vision of the show is clear and the characters are well-drawn, finding stories to sustain the show is never a problem. First of all, characters are the reason an audience tunes into a show. Plot is just the machinery which gives those characters a way to interact.

Audiences are so familiar with the FORM or STRUCTURE of a show that they can generally tune into their favourite one, a sitcom for instance, watch the first minute — which typically is an establishing joke, may or may not have anything to do with the plot but it reminds the audience who the characters are and what their attitudes are — and find themselves drawn into a relationship. Then the next thing that happens is that the problem is set up and we know who the central character is for that episode. Well, time to zap, because you know that if you come back at about 15 minutes past the hour the real fun starts which is the second act, a seven minute set-piece, where all hell breaks loose and all comedy ensues. So that's what you come back for.

By now you're probably asking yourselves, if I conceive a good show and execute it well, what else could I possibly need to have a long-running success? CASTING.

CASTING

Let's talk about casting for a bit. "**Cheers**" would have been a completely different show, and probably not the success it was, without the charm and comic talent of Ted Danson. Carol O'Connor, for example, Archie Bunker, was known for playing movie heavies before someone got him to read for the role of Archie Bunker. Larry Hagman was a sitcom character-actor before he was cast as J.R. Ewing. Lucille Ball's career had been mostly playing supporting roles in steamy B-movies before she was cast in "**I Love Lucy**" — I mean, could you imagine anyone else playing those roles? That's called owning a role.

> " *Characters are the reason an audience tunes into a show. Plot is just the machinery which gives those characters a way to interact.* "

Chemistry counts for a lot in casting. Shelley Long was a perfect foil for Ted Danson and an undeniable element of the show's success. Her departure at the height of the wave of success could have spelled doom for the show had the producers not come up with an interesting replacement, a relatively unknown actress called Kirstie Alley. She came in and provided an entirely new angle to the show, what they called "**Cheers Part II**". It renewed the show and the audience's interest in the show for another five years. That was great casting.

This is a particularly interesting time right now, by the way, in terms of television casting opportunities. With the down-turn in the film business worldwide, there are many 'name' actors, established film actors, who up until now wouldn't have considered doing television but who are now available, and interested in TV. Now's a good time. The casting of a film star in a series is considered an event and generates immediate audience and media interest.

So, I've got a great cast, I've got great scripts, I've got the best people working on it and we're on the air and we're in the middle of the first season. What's the deal? I mean, am I out of 'development hell' or not? What's left between me and a long-running successful television series? I hate to say it, but no matter how talented we are, how good a job we're doing, what sign we were born under, it all comes down to luck. The timing of the show, the mood of the country, world events, your time slot, the way the show's marketed, an executive turn-over at the network.

I said at the beginning that by the end of this talk we'd know if there was a formula for successful long-running TV series. There it is. Concept, execution, casting and luck.

Not a very scientific formula, but what's encouraging is that it's attainable. It's certainly been proven. In the end, the best we can do is the best we can do. And in my view, there are some real heroes showing us how well it can be done, people like Steven Bochco who's a consummate stylist, always pushing the boundaries of TV, who's given us such classy dramas as "**Hill Street Blues**" and "**LA Law**". Diane English who's one of the finest social satirists working in American TV, the creator of "**Murphy Brown**". Glen and Les Charles, two of the finest joke-smiths, who have created such classics as "**Cheers**" and "**Taxi**". Matt Williams, who uses craftsmanship and strong family values to create shows around stand-up comedians like "**Roseanne**" and "**The Cosby Show**". And Tim Allen in "**Home Improvement**".

Their dialogue has the ring of authenticity to it. Their comedy comes from keenly observed human behaviour and their pathos is derived from genuine honest emotion and a profound understanding of the universal human experience.

In the end the road to successful television begins with the choices that we, as writers, make from the start. I encourage all of you to write the kind of television that you'd like to watch, that moves you, that makes you excited, that makes you passionate. It won't make the development process any less hellish but it will make it a lot more bearable, and with luck it might just lead to success. So, *bonne chance*.

* * * * *

Additional information provided to the participants by Jason Brett included the following:

I. FOUR COMMON COMPONENTS OF SUCCESSFUL SERIES TELEVISION

1) CONCEPT
   - character(s)
   - theme
   - tone
       format/genre
       setting or environment

2) EXECUTION
   - vision /arcing the season's characters
   - production

3) CASTING
   - right actor for the role
   - chemistry
   - bonafide stars
   - stand-up comedians

4) LUCK
   - timing
   - programming / marketing
   - pre-empting / world events

II. FORMER TELEVISION SERIES NOW BEING PRODUCED AS FEATURE FILMS

"Maverick"
"The Fugitive"
"Addams Family Values"
"The Flintstones"
"Beverly Hillbillies"
"Dennis the Menace"
"F-Troop"
"Casper the Ghost"
"Hawaii Five-O"

"Wild, Wild West"
"Star Trek - VII"

*** This list does not include the following film adaptations of famous "Saturday Night Live" sketches, either currently in production, or previously produced.

"Wayne's World - II"
"The Coneheads"
"Blues Brothers"

III. TOP PRIME-TIME PROGRAMS

National rankings for the Top 20 prime-time network programs for total households and the Top 10 programe ranked by demographics for the week ending May 30.

Total households

Rank	Program	Network	Air Day	Air Time	Rating
1	Daytime Emmys	ABC	Wed	9:00	16.4
2	Roseanne	ABC	Tue.	9:00	16.0
3	Hurricane Andrew	NBC	Mon.	9:30	15.7
4	Beverly Hillbillies	CBS	Mon.	8:00	15.2
Tie	Seinfeld	NBC	Thu.	9:30	15.2
6	20/20 Anniversary	ABC	Tue.	9:30	15.1
7	Northem Exposure	CBS	Mon.	10:00	14.7
8	Home Improvement	ABC	Wed.	8:00	14.5
9	Love, Honor & Obey	CBS	Mon.	9:00	14.2
10	Designing Women	CBS	Mon.	9:00	14.2
11	Rescue 011	CBS	Tue.	8:00	14.0
12	Prime Time	ABC	Thu.	10:00	13.8
13	60 Minutes	CBS	Sun.	7:00	13.6
14	20/20	ABC	Fri.	10:00	13.2
15	Coach	ABC	Wed.	8:30	12.8
16	Cheers	NBC	Thu.	9:00	12.6
Tie	LA Law	NBC	Thu.	10:00	12.6
18	Half House	ABC	Tue.	8:00	12.0
Tie	Murder, She Wrote	CBS	Sun.	8:00	11.8
20	Hangin' with Mr. Cooper	ABC	Tue.	8:30	11.8

Women 18-49

Group size: 60.870.000

Rank	Program	Rating
1	Roseanne	12.9
2	Daytime Emmys	12.6
3	Seinfeld	12.0
4	20/20 Anniversary	11.5
5	Hurricane Andrew Story	11.2
6	Designing Women	10.9
Tie	Northern Exposure	10.9
8	Home Improvement	10.2
9	Rescue: 011	9.9
10	LA Law	9.6

Men 18-49

Group size: 69.450.000

Rank	Program	Rating
1	Seinfeld	9.9
2	Hurricane Andrew Story	8.3
3	Home Improvement	8.3
4	Northern Exposure	8.1
5	Cheers	8.0
6	Roseanne	7.5
7	Beverly Hillbillies	7.4
8	20/20 Anniversary	7.1
9	Simpsons	7.0
10	A Fish Called Wanda	6.7

Teens 12-17

Group Size: 20.110.000

Rank	Program	Rating
1	Fresh Prince	12.6
2	Martin	11.0
3	Blossom	11.7
4	Roseanne	10.7
Tie	Simpsons	10.7
6	90210: bchind scenes	10.3
7	Melrose Place	10.0
8	Hangin' With Mr. Cooper	9.1
9	Hurricane Andrew Story	8.8
10	In Living Color	8.7

Kids 2-11

Group size: 36.870.000

Rank	Program	Rating
1	Dinosaurs	13.9
2	Step by Stop	12.0
3	Full House	11.7
4	Simpsons	11.1
5	Hangin' With Mr. Cooper	10.8
6	Home free	10.4
7	Family Matters	10.1
8	Martin	9.7
9	Blossom	8.8
10	Roseanne	8.5

Source: A.C. Nielsen Co.

IV. SOME 1993 FALL COMEDY PICK-UPS

"**Buddies**" — The lives of two best friends change when one of them gets married and has a baby.

"**Couples**" — One-camera comedy about three couples in a Manhattan apartment building.

"**George**" — Boxer George Foreman as a Junior High guidance counselor.

"**Grace Under Fire**" — A single mother taking various jobs to support three small children.

"**Little Niagara**" — A New York detective becomes the sheriff of a small town

"**The Lang Game**" — Ensemble comedy as a pro golfer is forced to become a country club pro.

"**Sister, Sister**" — Twin teenage girls are reunited at age 13, forming an extended family with one's single mother and the other's widowed father.

"**Dave's World**" — A series based on the work of a syndicated columnist.

"**Incredi-Girl**" — Heroine of a comic book-style TV show whose off-camera life is falling apart.

"**South Central**" — A single mother raises her three kids in South Central L.A.

"**Family Album**" — A family moves from California back to Philadelphia to be near their aging parents.

"**It Had to Be You**" — About a high-class Boston publisher who marries a blue collar guy.

"**The Boys**" — A thirtysomething writer and his girlfriend move into the house of a deceased man and inherit his elderly friends.

"**Tall Hopes**" — A Philadelphia family dreams of fame and fortune in the form of the 5-foot 7-inch son as a high-school basketball star.

"**The Building**" — Ensemble comedy set in a Chicago apartment building.

"**Island Guy**" — A naive Pacific Islander paddles to the States and finds himself living with a yuppie couple.

"**Big Wave Dave's**" — Three middle-aged guys junk life in Chicago and open a Hawaii surf shop.

"**Those Two**" — A writer whose well-ordered life is upset when his friend leaves her husband and moves in with him.

"**Trailer Park**" — About a resident in a tacky Florida trailer park living next to onetime country club types who find themselves there as well.

V. SOME 1993 DRAMA PICK-UPS

"**Birdland**" — Chief psychiatrist at a major metropolitan hospital.

"**Bodyguards**" — Light action show about bodyguards working for a personal security agency.

"**Divas**" — Singing quartet struggling to make it as performers and balance their personal lives.

"**Doors**" — Sci-fi pilot dealing with a doctor and alien warrior travelling through "doors" into different alien worlds each week.

"**Do the Strand**" — Owner of a Florida security business who becomes entangled with an impetuous young woman.

"**Lois & Clark: The New Adventures of Superman**" — Series tracing the more personal aspect of the hopeless Clark-Lois-Superman triangle.

"**Missing Persons**" — Chicago's missing persons unit in a series blending drama with elements of reality shows.

"**My So-Called Life**" — Ensemble coming-of-age drama from the pov of a teenager.

"**NYPD Blues**" — Single-lead cop show being written as TV's first PG-13 series.

"**On the Street**" — About a tough but compassionate foot-patrol officer.

"**Profiles**" — A hybrid talk show/drama, the show takes a talk format and dramatizes it moving inside the fictional guests' minds through flashbacks and exploring action beyond the cameras.

"**Harts of the West**" — A Chicago family that buys a dude ranch and moves west.

"**Arty Hanks**" — A family drama about a female sheriff of a small Arkansas town.

"**Greyhounds**" — A quartet of retired lawmen fighting crime in San Diego.

"**Summer**" — Ensemble serial about four couples and their "very single male friend" living in Summer, Mass.

"**Shenandoah**" — Two-hour pilot about a pair of Southern families at the time of the Civil War.

VI. TV MOVIE ACT STRUCTURE

- Writer's First Draft runs 115-120 pages.
- Submission First Draft runs 110 pages.
- TV scripts are 1 1/2 pages per minute.

Act I (20-25 pages)

- Establish characters for most of the act.
- Set up the problem at the end of the act.
- Generally, a story has two problems:
  Primary problem
  Secondary problem (subplot)

Act II (15-17 pages)

- Heighten/intensify the problem.
- End each act with a mini-climax.

Act III (15-17 pages)

- Explode the problem with a confrontation, a major crisis.
- Hit critical mass at end of act.
- End act with a mini-climax.

Act IV (15-17 pages)

- Aftermath of the intensified problem.
- Characters are desperate, forlorn, sure of failure: having lost faith, solving the problem seems impossible.

Act V (15-17 pages)

- The resolution begins.
- Explain how to solve the problem.
- Hope in solving/resolving the problem is restored.
- Characteres put resolution into motion.
- End act with a mini-climax.

Act VI (8-10 pages)

- Continue action leading to the resolution.
- At end of act, foreshadow the resolution.
- End act with a mini-climax.

Act VII (8-10 pages)

- Climax takes place halfway through act.
- Resolution and denouement are played out.

VII. HOUR LONG EPISODIC TELEVISION STRUCTURE

- Writer's First Draft runs 68-72 pages.
- Submission First Draft runs 60 pages.

Act I (12-15 pages)

- Establish problem(s) — primary and secondary.
- Problem asks a question:
  "Will McGyver save the girl?"
  "Will Magnum get the kidnapper?"
- End act with a mini-climax.

Act II (10-14 pages)

- Complicate problem. (Obstacles)
- End act with a mini-climax.

Act III (10-15 pages)

- Intensify problem. (More obstacles)
- End act with a mini-climax. (It doesn't look good for our hero…)

Act IV (10-12 pages)

- Resolve the problem / Our hero prevails.

Tag (1-5 pages, if used)

- Typically, a light-hearted commentary on the problem, or a moral.

VIII. HALF-HOUR EPISODIC TELEVISION STRUCTURE

- Writer's First Draft varies in length according to show.

Teaser (1-3 pages)

- Typically, witty banter and jokes that put the characters into their relationships and environment. (Does not necessarily relate to the episode's story.)

Act I (15-25 pages)

- Sets up the problem(s), or "hook": establishes who the episode's major character is, and their problem.
  "Lucy wants to audition for the amateur talent show at the club, but Ricky won't let her."
- Set up subplot.
  "Lucy and Ethel audition in disguise, and get into show."
  End with complication, cliff-hanger or act break.
  "Rickey and Fred find out what their wives have done, and decide to play along and let the wives make fools of themselves."

Act II (15-25 pages)

- "The Block Scene" — a seven minute, extended set piece of physical or behavioral comedy where things go from bad to worse for the lead character(s).
  "Lucy and Ethel perform and everything that can go wrong, does — including Ricky finding out."

Tag (1-3 pages)

- Like the teaser, this may or may not relate to the story. Typically, it's a moral and a big laugh.
  "Lucy learns her lesson... but finds out there's going to be another amateur show and conspires with Ethel to try again...)

IX. THE TEN BASIC SITCOM PLOTS

1) The bet

Can a character give up a vice, or "Whose job is harder, let's switch and see!" ("Fine, you're on!" "Fine"!)

2) The guest star

A celebrity or public figure comes on the show as themselves. ("Oh my god, it's Michael Jackson — I'm gonna die!")

3) The mistaken identity

Twins, or other nutty coincidence causes big ruckus. ("Oh no, if you're not my personal trainer, that means your my boss' niece!")

4) Risky business

Character borrows car or throws party when forbidden to. ("Really, Dad — we were rehearsing for the school play!")

5) The big misunderstanding

Overheard snippet of conversation wreaks havoc. ("A surprise party? For me? So that's why you're calling all those male strippers!")

6) Two dates for the same night

"Character has already said yes to the bookworm when the hunk gives her a call. ("Uh — wait right here. I'll be right back.")

7) Jealousy

Siblings/friends fight over dream guy/girl. ("Give me my hairbrush back!" "Give me my Frankie back!")

8) The feared dinner guest

Boss or mother-in-law comes to visit and thing go awry.
("Would you like more wine — whoops!" "Here, — let me, whoops!")

9) The big lie

Fib turns into preposterous explanation.
("Oh — uh, this is my, um, sister... and the reason she speaks only Cantonese is, um...")

10) The forgotten birthday

Oafish spouse has memory lapse.
("I remember, honey. It's... yesterday?")
... And if all else fails, put a man in a dress.

X. PLOT

Plot is the story device we use to put our characters in motion and explore their relationships.

The average situation comedy plot is simplistic, unimaginative and cliched.

"Cheers", the Amcrican comedy series set in a neighborhood bar, not only ended its eleven year run as one of the most celebrated and top rated shows ever, it also set standards of excellence in television writing, year after year.

Compare the plots of some of the more memorable episodes of "Cheers", with the list following it of the ten basic plots you're likely to see on the average, generic sitcom.

Examples of some of the "Cheers" plots

"Coach's Daughter" — Lisa is engaged to an inconsiderate bore. It's the best one can do, she claims. But Coach is a father who sees only beauty in a daughter. He inspires Lisa to send the lout packing.

"**Peterson Crusoe**" — When the spot on his X-ray is negative, Norm wants to celebrate by starting over in Bora Bora. But just as the Cheers regulars are comparing him to Gauguin, he is found hiding in the bar's back office.

"**Fear is My Co-Pilot**" — The plane is falling and the pilot looks dead. "You and me married?", Sam says to Diane. "Why didn't I ask you when I had the chance?" She says, "At least we're going together…" The pilot recovers.

"**The Proposal**" — Because Diane wants a romantic proposal (not over the telephone), Sam arranges a moonlight sail. "What I'm trying to say is, will you marry me?", he asks. Diane pauses and answers, "No". Sam throws her overboard.

"**The Gift of the Woodi**" — Woody writes a birthday song for Kelly because he can't afford a present. "Kelly, Kelly, Kelly, Kelly", goes the chorus. "Woody, that was beautiful", Kelly says. "So, where my gift?"

"**Days of Wine and Neurosis**" — Sam finds Rebecca drunk and proclaiming that she doesn't love her fiance, and wants Sam instead. Belting out a few bars of "We've got Tonight", she passes out.

XI. MOST COMMON OCCUPATIONS ON PRIME TIME

1. Police Officer
2. Lawyer
3. Doctor
4. Restauranteur
5. Television reporter/host
6. Nurse
7. Newspaper editor/reporter/columnist
8. Television writer/producer
9. Interior decorator
9. Coach
9. Radio host/disc jockey

There is a three-way tie for the ninth position.

MOST COMMON OCCUPATIONS IN THE UNITED STATES

1. Salesman/sales woman
2. Teacher
3. Secretary
4. Accountant/book-keeper
5. Truck driver
6. Cashier
7. Janitor
8. Nurse
9. Cook
10. Engineer

Source: The US Bureau of Labor Statistics. 1992

XII. THE SIX PHASES OF TELEVISION PRODUCTION

1) Wild enthusiasm.
2) Disillusionment.
3) Panic…
4) Search for the guilty.
5) Punish the innocent (as in, blame the writer).
6) Reward the non-involved.

* * * * *

Typo seen in the television column of the Los Angeles Times:

"… the network brass stated they were pleased, and planned no changes at this time in the weakly television schedule."

49

HOW TO WRITE A HIT

CARYN MANDABACH

President of the Carsey/Warner Company in Los Angeles. Supervising Executive on their hugely successful sitcoms "Roseanne" and "The Cosby Show".

I was the first producer of "**The Cosby Show**". That was quite remarkable because it was shot in New York, and I lived in L.A. We had to move the production to New York which was very extreme because New York was notoriously bad to shoot in. The studio, which was run down, was in a horrifying neighbourhood in Brooklyn, and it had all the worst possible conditions. That's where my career really took off. After that I left producing and became an executive and did a number of other shows like "**Roseanne**" and "**A Different World**". So I'm going to be talking about hits and the structure of a hit and what makes a hit. We've made two big fat smash hits so I will talk to you about the particulars from those that I think might help you.

As you know, the situation comedy is a uniquely American form, like tap dancing or barbecue or breast implants. We are famous for it, we've been famous for it since the '50s, and while many aspects of it have evolved since the '50s, a lot has remained the same. For the most part the sitcom aims to have us laugh at ourselves and the world around us. It doesn't want to challenge us or cause us to think. People come home from a hard day and they just don't want to be challenged. They want to be entertained, and that's our job, and it's a hard job because you have to tell stories and you have to change the stories and make them interesting all the time. But it's important to talk a little about history before getting into the present, so I'm going to talk about the history of the hit as a way of getting to the present day.

The situation comedy form breaks into two groups: the family show and the ensemble show. In the '50s there were, I think, four shows which spoke brilliantly for the medium in it's infancy: "**I Love Lucy**", "**The Honeymooners**", a show you might not have seen called "**You'll Never Get Rich**", and "**The Jack Benny Show**". The first two are family shows and the second two are ensemble shows. But all of them have one significant element of a hit and here it is:

PUT A FUNNY PERSON IN THE CENTRE OF A SHOW

Lucille, Jackie Gleason, Phil Silvers and Jack Benny all created hit characters, and were funny people.

Another important element however is:

COMMENTARY ON SOME IMPORTANT
ASPECT OF THE CULTURE

Lucy spoke to the longing that women in the '50s had to be special, to be heard. Even though she was whining a lot of the time, what she wanted was to be in show business. She had a dream and that was an important thing — to be articulate. Though she was helpless and never really got what she wanted, at least she articulated her dreams. Similarly, those of you who remember Jackie Gleason remember that he was loud and boisterous and angry, but of course it was his wife Alice who had all the wisdom in the house and **that** was something new.

In addition to having the aforementioned elements, "**You'll Never Get Rich**", which starred a brilliant comedian, Phil Silvers, and "**The Jack Benny Show**" also serve to illustrate the third most important element of a great series:

MAKE THE STORIES THEMSELVES FRESH AND FUNNY

"**You'll Never Get Rich**" featured a fast-talking, gambling con-man character named Sgt. Bilko who was nonetheless a champion against the faceless bureaucracy of the military, and it was a lot of fun to watch Bilko every week do something incredibly clever. In one episode I remember his boss was very annoying so he actually managed to get his boss to play golf with the then president Eisenhower. And it was wonderful. You never saw Eisenhower but you saw a look-alike of Eisenhower and that was very fresh and very smart in the '50s.

"**The Jack Benny Show**" used an ancient literary convention to tell its stories, and that was 'the show within a show'. The premise of that show was that Jack was playing a vain, stingy, prideful violinist who was the star of a variety show each week and he was the helpless victim of that process. It was very self-referential, it was a new way of telling stories on television. But it was also an old way of telling stories, because it was Shakespearean.

Before moving on I'm going to stop and make another sweeping generalization, which is:

HIT SITCOM CHARACTERS ARE COMPLEX

Lucy is strong and weak, Jackie talks big but he's afraid, Sgt. Bilko is conniving but protective of his men and Jack may be the star of the show but he has really no power over it. So don't be afraid to write complex characters.

Now we move on to the '60s. The same rules apply but more can be observed. Today I want to talk to you about four shows. They are: "**Leave It To Beaver**", "**Ozzie and Harriet**", "**The Dick Van Dyke Show**" and "**The Flintstones**". They all have something relevant for you.

"**Leave it to Beaver**" was the quintessential family show and it was unique for two reasons. One was the point of view. This was the first time in television where the point of view was through the eyes of a seven-year-old child, Beaver Cleaver. It was his show and we saw all the stories through the eyes of Beaver. Childrens' stories at that time had not yet been accurately, or in fact at all, represented on television, so that was a breakthrough hit.

It was also a breakthrough hit because it presented an idealized version of the '60s family. Nobody really lived like the Cleavers, I assure you, and yet we liked to see this idealized situation; it was the tone that was new. You have to find your tone. It has to be a unique tone, it has to be something that rings true. That was an idealized tone and everybody went "Mmmm", so the tone and the point of view were special in "**Beaver**".

"**Ozzie and Harriet**" was about the Nelson family. Ozzie and Harriet Nelson were real people, famous show-business people and they had a couple of kids and they did a show about their lives. They actually portrayed themselves in the sitcom to the extent that they replicated their own home for the set and they had replications of their friends and their relatives. It was very bizarrely self-referential; scary, if you think about it. But I think it was a milestone. To watch little Ricky Nelson and his brother grow up was vaguely voyeuristic, I thought. But again it had a new tone and that leads to this point that wherever possible you should:

TRY TO FIND A FRESH ANGLE OR NEW POINT OF VIEW FOR YOUR STORY TELLING

In the '60s we also have the "**The Dick Van Dyke Show**" and "**The Flintstones**", and these are classics for different reasons. "**The Dick Van Dyke Show**" had the distinction of being the first show to take place in two different settings: the home and the office. They were equally important. This was new, this was fresh: it was both family and ensemble sitcom. It was also unique in that it portrayed relatable, believable characters in unusual situations. They were relatable in that he was a comedy writer, he was a nice man, he was a family man but he had this extremely unusual situation in that he had to appease this insanely difficult star, Alan Brady. Alan Brady posed an obstacle and I suggest that it's generally a good idea to have an obstacle somewhere in your story. And the other great thing about it was that it also presented a nearly flawless combination of writing and performing.

This brings me to another thought:

WHEN DOING A PILOT WHY NOT WRITE FOR YOUR IDEAL CAST?

The writers didn't know at first that these actors were going to be so brilliant. Nobody knew that Mary Tyler Moore was going to be so fresh, so extremely relatable, so very real as a '60s modern woman. But if you can, imagine who your stars are and write for them. You might not get them but you might as well go for it.

Finally in the '60s **"The Flintstones"** was a hit because it was a stylistic breakthrough. It was a virtual remake of **"The Honeymooners"** — basically, Fred Flintstone was the Jackie Gleason character, his friend Barney was the Art Carney character. But what made it different of course was that it was animated and it was in prime time, so it thus afforded the opportunity for unusual jokes like the bird underneath the sink as the garbage disposal. So there's not much to learn here except if you're in the mood you can create:

A NEW VISUAL STYLE

Why not? You've got technology, some of the things you could do cheaply. I mean some shows are totally made on visual style. **"Miami Vice"** was frankly not that interesting a show, but it had a really cool visual style. In other words you don't have to worry too much about your content if your style is really cool.

Moving on to the '70s, they gave us a truly important family show but also it was the golden age of the ensemble show. The family show, **"All in the Family"**, offered the first really topical sitcom and a real break in style from the idealized tones of the '60s. Here is the first sitcom where real issues such as race, sexuality, political correctness are depicted. But most importantly, here we find the first truly great character study in Archie Bunker, who was of course a loud, conservative, stubborn, obnoxious person who changes. This is something important to know. He changes considerably throughout the course of the series. His wife, Edith, of course also changed from a dingbat to a deeply principled, assertive woman. This series therefore reinforces the notion that:

IF YOU CREATE CHARACTERS WITH THE POTENTIAL FOR CHANGE YOU ARE DOING THE BEST THING YOU CAN POSSIBLY DO

When I talked about complex characters before I was actually referring to a complexity which gives them a comic dynamic. This is very important: if they can't change, if they can't feel something new and different, there's nothing poignant. You'll stop caring very soon. So that's what "**All in the Family**" actually did.

Now the ensemble shows. In "**MASH**", a classic ensemble piece of the '70s, we have the brutally real world of the Korean war contrasted against the raucous behaviour of the doctors, nurses and administrators who are simply trying to survive. That's all they're doing. So their humour in this case comes from their constant denial of their predicament. This is again a classic form of humour. But what happened on this series was that a very new thing was born — it was a very dark tone. You know, if you are making love and the bullets are flying over your head, that's a new sound and it was brand new to TV. Also what was brand new was that they took a movie and put it on TV as a series; that was the first time they had done that as well. So another thing to say therefore is:

DON'T BE AFRAID TO CREATE A NEW TONE

It would make you stand out, it would make everybody hear you differently.

"**The Mary Tyler Moore Show**" sported the first female lead in an ensemble show. As the first single working woman character on television her cultural impact during the '70s was immeasurable. There were a whole bunch of shows where the women were just there, they were not important. But she was the lead, she was on her own, she was single! She was in her thirties! Imagine that in the '70s! It was quite a breakthrough show. This was character-based comedy at its best. These characters were living and breathing people, you knew them, you were sure you knew them, and beyond having contrasting personality traits which set one against the other, the thing about "**The Mary Tyler Moore Show**" and the characters was that they were all flawed. They all had something wrong with them.

But the most important thing about this show, aside from the flaws, was that Mary was hugely likeable. I don't remember before or after a character as likeable as Mary was in that show. You wanted to hug her. So the thing to remember here is:

NEVER UNDERESTIMATE THE IMPORTANCE
OF HAVING A LIKEABLE CHARACTER

Somewhere, somebody's got to be wildly relatable, vulnerable, like-able. Give the audience something to hang on to.

In the '70s another important breakthrough hit was called "**Soap**". It could have been a parody but it wasn't. Instead it was a deft mix of funny bits, clever plots, and reflective moments. The plots were so clever, they had Martians, they had murders but they were always interesting. The key thing about Susan Harris, a remarkable writer who also created "**The Golden Girls**", was her reflective moments. She had at the core of that show two sisters, and the two sisters would sit and have a cup of coffee and even though insane things were happening around them, that cup of coffee and the fact that they would always talk about things that women talk about was very, very important. So her reflective moments, particularly for women, struck a big chord and again through her work with "**The Golden Girls**" you can pretty much always see that they talk about the same things: sex, food and death. But, you know, these are not bad subjects for comedy.

OK, so moving on to the '80s. The '80s featured "**The Cosby Show**", of course, and its antidote "**Married with Children**". And "**Cheers**" as the classic ensemble piece of the generation. Now "**The Cosby Show**" was interesting because, for a number of reasons, it was very light on story. A goldfish dies, a sister makes a bad shirt for her brother, a young child wants to stay up late. Those are not really stories, they're really key scenes. And that's what Cosby wanted to do, he didn't really want to have, "Oh! two dates for the prom. Who'll she go out with?" So he broke with that story form and made it a slice of life.

Another reason why it was different was that the parents depicted on television prior to 1984 were the goofy ones, the kids were smart; when Cosby came he showed that parents were in charge. The other thing was that Cliff and Clair were wild for each other. They were totally romantic, they were sexy. We never saw a married couple in bed before, hugging and kissing — this was new. These are simple things but they were new and it's the simple things that you should think about, making them fresh. You should look at television like a map and you should say "What's missing? Something's not here, I need to fill in this blank."

Another simple thing Cosby picked out was that the people were happy. This was a throwback to the '60s because it presented a totally idealized version of the family. Claire was an attorney, she had five children and she didn't have a housekeeper, yet there was not one sock ever on that set. It was all perfect, they solved every single problem. It was a conscious decision to have an idealized version of a family. But probably the most important thing about "**The Cosby Show**" was that the cultural commentary was enormous. It referenced the fact that this family was black but it emphasized the similarities in our culture as opposed to the differences, always a good thing to do. If you're going to make a cultural commentary about disparate elements in your culture, talk about the similarities, pull people together, give them something to hang on to. It makes us feel good about ourselves. Don't underestimate that.

"**Married with Children**" takes Cosby's idealized life and rips the guts out of it, turns it upside down. The Bundy family is crude, they're cynical, they're mean but they're wildly entertaining. Why? Because we were up to here with the lovely family setting by the time "**Married with Children**" came along. What I liked about that show more than anything was that the writers were not afraid to be different. They were writing about the misery of marriage. As opposed to the idealized Cosby world of the wonders of unending love.

Finally we have "**Cheers**", a successful mix of characters who mainly talked about the struggle between the sexes, a hugely important *Zeitgeist* for the '80s. So like Mary and Dick van Dyke before them, the characters were brilliantly drawn — from the acid-tongued waitress to the illogical innocent to the deadpan intellectual characters. But of course they were also brilliantly cast. This was again an example of genius writing and genius casting. So remember anyone can say they want to do a show set in a bar or in a supermarket or in a hairdressing salon or in a meat shop or in a hotel, but it's really through craft, through patient writing and re-writing that it succeeds. The more you work it, the better it gets. A final thought then:

BE FLEXIBLE

Don't fall in love with anything and if you do, don't marry it. There will be a more dynamic way to talk about the character, there will always be a better story, there will be a pithier comment, there will be a fresher tone, there will be a newer style. And always remember that, in the act of creation, God is in the details.

One more thing:

FEEL FREE TO IGNORE EVERYTHING I HAVE JUST SAID. BECAUSE THE TRUTH IS — EVERY HIT IS A MIRACLE.

DESPERATION AS THE MOTHER OF INVENTION

JEFFREY LEWIS

Emmy-award winning writer and producer, Jeffrey Lewis started as story editor on "Hill Street Blues", then worked as producer and finally executive producer for its 6th and 7th seasons. He has also created other long-running series for NBC.

"**Hill Street Blues**" was probably the first drama in American TV history to use team writing so extensively. The show had from 12 to 16 main characters and several more recurring characters, each of which had a history, each one of which we hoped was going someplace in their personal lives. We produced 22 hours more or less per year on a production schedule that allowed 7 days ordinarily to shoot a 47' show and the fact was that we didn't have a lot of time to do these scripts.

But we were doing a show which wouldn't have survived unless the writing was lively and the character development was interesting. It didn't have much action, it didn't have sex-appeal in traditional ways, it didn't have the things that normally hook an audience. What it had was the possiblity of presenting a vibrant world and we felt a need, in a very competitive environment where if people stop watching a show it goes off the air, to make the shows as vibrant as possible.

On a show this complicated it was felt that the most important function was to have the stories right and the structure of each episode correct, because if the dialogue was rather lame or dull or the characters' attitudes seemed flat or uninteresting, those things could be relatively easily fixed. But if the structure of the entire hour was dull or flat or didn't work or the character development made no sense or the story was just stupid, that really meant that even if there was some really fine writing in the episode, probably that fine writing would never see the screen.

So the way we worked when I joined the show in the second season, the two people who started the show, Michael Kozoll and Steven Bochco, would sit in a room in the morning, three or four mornings, deciding what would be some good stories — what they had seen in the newspapers, what their aunt had told them, what they'd heard on TV in Philadelphia, whatever. Usually for, say, a run of four episodes we'd have two or three main stories and then in each episode NBC required that there be one story which began and ended in that episode so that the casual viewer would have something to relate to. So they'd come up with these stories and outline them step-by-step on a blackboard, divided into four columns for the four so-called acts of our show. The first column would have the beats — the six or seven scenes of the first act and so on through the four acts.

When they had this blackboard sufficiently full, and on the reverse side of the board perhaps notes on where we were going through the four episode series, Tony Yerkovich, Mike Wagner and I would talk through this structure with Steven and Michael, making a few changes along the way but not necessarily that many. We'd talk through scene by scene — if anyone had ideas as to how a scene might go, they would say "But how about this, what if we did this?" If there was agreement in the room that 'this seems to work', if people got a visceral charge out of an idea, usually that would be remembered and find its way into the script. If it seemed lame or didn't seem interesting, there would be long periods of silence until something fresh was thought up.

At a certain point, and I don't remember when, we began taping these sessions on audio-cassette, act by act, one cassette per act, and when these sessions were done — they usually took a day or day and a half — the person who was then going to attempt to write the portion of the teleplay based on this material, would take the cassette home and listen to it, maybe make notes on it or just contemplate it or throw it out. Most people used them but there was no obligation to do so. And from that group consensus as to where the episode ought to be going, those people writing the teleplay would attempt to write it.

Typically, in the first pass at writing the teleplay, one person would write the first act, one person would write the second act, a third person would write the third act and that's how the show was staffed. We tried to have four people around, each of whom could write an act of a script each week. And the hope was that the amount of time spent in meetings and going over the script and structure would give people enough of a shared understanding of what was going on, when one put the four pieces together they wouldn't look like a camel but would look like a cow, that they'd bear some resemblance to the original intention that everybody had when we were sitting in the room.

> " *Concision of dialogue we thought was important.* "

In reality, this was usually not the case. It was a rare case when the script one got back cohered, because almost inevitably someone had found something impossible to do and had fudged it. Or had got excited about a scene and their act wound up being 19 pages. And then somebody else had got excited about another scene and their act was 19 pages also, so we wound up with a script that would have shot an hour and a half of film. Or people would simply have difficulties with things or would have had varying understandings. So when we came together to look this stuff over, the most senior people would furrow their brows and we'd get in a room and talk about it again and the second time perhaps we would divide the work differently.

The second time perhaps someone would say "Well, why don't you take the story that goes through the court?". That would typically be to me, because I'd spent time in court rooms and knew better than anyone else how they worked. Michael Wagner, who was good at crazy characters, he liked people on the edge and wrote them in a nice, endearing way, he'd probably do that story next time around and smooth all the beats of that story. Tony Yerkovich liked to write, among others, right-wingers and gang kids, Howard Hunter and Jesus Martinez; it gave him a great deal of pleasure, and he would tend to do those with some excitement and some irony. We would go out for whatever amount of time, maybe a couple of days, and do that work and come back.

Then probably we had stories which to each of us now felt better beat by beat, which had a certain more nuanced consistency, but which may not have been knitted together very well. They might seem now to be rather in isolation from one another, whereas what we were trying to create was an intensely felt environment of community. That is, the station house and the people in it. This was a world where everything was going on at once, where everything was bubbling up. What we wanted was the feeling that at some point everyone's story was bumping up against everyone else's and maybe having some resonance and some thematic significance as a result of that, in terms of what this day in this station house was like, this ghetto-world, what was going on in it in the course of a day.

> *" We were trying to be as concise as possible so that as much could happen in as many different moods and colours as we could get into 47 minutes. "*

At that point one could say one forgets about team writing and one person — probably a senior person — has to make sense of the whole thing. Subsequent stages of writing this single script might be along the lines of some scenes still stink or are hard to do, or aren't working. Or one of the acts is really slow. We then did polish work on dialogue. Concision of dialogue we thought was important, we were constantly winnowing down the dialogue, except if it was funny when we'd try to make more of it so it would last as long as possible. But generally speaking we were trying to be as concise as possible so that as much could happen in as many different moods and colours as we could get into 47 minutes.

There would be other specific cases when one writer would undertake to patch things up. An actor would come in and say 'This stinks, I wouldn't say this', or 'You didn't give me anything to say, you suck', so we would try to make amends, make peace and do it right. There were specific people who tended to cater for specific needs. Again, I tended to write when Veronica Hamel couldn't say this long word, because it was some legal term. Steven Bochco was married to the actress who played the ex-wife of the captain, so he had some incentive to make sure that her scenes were good. And so on.

And then, of course, there's the great moment when the director comes on board, which is usually late in the writing process, although as the season wore on not so late because we were getting later and later in trying to get these scripts together. So sometimes the director would be around kind of twiddling his thumbs and making us feel uncomfortable for not having given him a script yet and at that point the director's concerns would be listened to. But this was a world in which directors had relatively little say, as opposed to the feature-film world where the directors are all and the writers scarcely listened to because they have little commercial impact on whether the film will make money or not — or at least so it is thought.

> " This was a world in which directors had relatively little say. "

In this process, in the intensive process of an ongoing long-running TV series, particularly one that was an ensemble series depending on a variety of characters and the snappiness of the writing and nuance of character (as opposed to a show which was simply dependent on Bruce Willis standing up there and smiling, in which case Bruce Willis would have the power), writers had a fair amount of power — a rare and wonderful thing for a writer. So the director would come in and say what he thought and we would typically say 'Well, that's because you haven't been here before, you don't know and so do it our way.' Of course, if we felt he was right we would try to accommodate that but generally speaking the shoe was on the other foot and I think all of us writers who were part of this process were very grateful for that. It also induced us to give up a little bit of our autonomy in favour of collective power.

I think that the most important thing regarding writers working as a team is that one musn't be afraid to rewrite. These things really need to be rewritten a lot, and it really is possible to make scripts better by continuing to work on them intensively and having more than one set of eyes working on them. There's some value in saying 'Look we're putting this show on, if people stop watching it, we're out of a job and this show's dead.' And what have we got to sell here? Well, we've got some characters that people like to watch and we have some jokes which seem to bear a relation to people's real lives, about living in big cities and trouble, and if we don't hold the audience minute by minute in a sort of visceral way, then we'll lose them and we'll start becoming like a lot of other shows. The writers have to say "We'd better make this work, we'd better make sure by the end of this act that people are going to come back after the commercial and watch the rest."

> " These things really need to be rewritten a lot, and it really is possible to make scripts better by continuing to work on them intensively and having more than one set of eyes working on them. "

Now, something about the uncomfortable or wonderful subject of money. On a "Hill Street Blues" script, practically everyone working on the show might get a credit, say, three people with a story credit and four people a teleplay credit. And all of those people were on the staff of the show, in one way or another. The executive producers were always writers as well as half the people with producer titles, and then "junior" writers who weren't producers were usually story editors or story consultants or whatever. All of us were getting well paid in our staff positions, more money than most of us imagined writers could get paid, and, in addition, we got paid to write the scripts.

The Writers Guild of America has minimums which have to be paid for writing a script and the minimums require that a writer for any portion of a script, even if they didn't write as much as half, has to be paid for the minimum established for half of it. Which meant that if there were four people writing the teleplay and in theory each person was responsible for a quarter of the script, each would be paid as if they were writing half. So this meant that it became very attractive for the people who were on the staff to have as many people as possible writing it, because you still got paid the same, even if four people did it instead of two.

This drove the parent company totally crazy, as you can imagine, because it was a big waste of money, supposedly. And there's some truth in this. I would bet anything that there is no production company in America now that would allow four writers to write a teleplay — or four credited writers — because the economics don't work any more. But in 1984 Ronald Reagan was President, people were borrowing against the future like crazy, money was flying around and this incentive without a doubt contributed to the good nature of writers asked to work together on close terms. It made us feel like part of a great conspiracy, writers who were figuring out a way to do well, in terms other than our private concerns of having the script be beautiful. We were kind of like middle-class guys doing well and I will confess that this process was very appealing. If you ignore it and expect writers to go into a room and do everything that they don't naturally want to do and in addition not pay them nicely or give them some other incentives to do it, they'll probably be grumpy.

> *" If we don't hold the audience minute by minute in a sort of visceral way, then we'll lose them. "*

So I'd say that within what budgets and circumstance will allow, if you want to encourage team writing, pay the people as well as you can and better than they can do elsewhere. I'm quite confident the results will be better. The same goes for the question of titles. All the titles were inflated, they all described more pompous functions than were in fact executed by the people given the titles. But why shouldn't you have a job description which makes you feel a little grander than what you're doing? It was another kind of cushy incentive to make you feel part of a privileged society that was making a good product and where people also recognised you in ways you hadn't been recognised before.

There were also some unexpected benefits of writing in this way. One is that it was possible to get a degree of universality into the project without losing a certain degree of particularity. I say this because it's very hard to write an intensely private story when there are so many people in the room, when there are so many eyes on the project. One tends to become part of the communal effort and get outside oneself more than otherwise, so the themes and outlooks tend to become a little more widely held by necessity in order to accommodate the various voices and talents and consciousnesses in the room. At the same time, by dividing the work and redividing the work and ultimately giving one person the opportunity of doing this or doing that, one doesn't necessarily lose the particularity that only one writer can bring to one scene. One wouldn't, I suppose, try to write a series called "**The Lonely Guy**" with seven people in the room. But nobody would probably want to watch that series.

Finally, I think this process encourages a sense of craftsmanship, which is useful, as opposed to authorship, as opposed to the feeling that writers have of 'us against the world', which can lead to alarmingly grotesque versions of that world, as well as genius versions. Here one thinks the project is outside oneself a little more, like hammering away at a sculpture on a cathedral rather than doing the whole thing. And certainly on a show trying to attract a wide audience by having a wide variety of character and situations, there's some usefulness in having a writing environment which reflects the world you are trying to create.

> " *It was possible to get a degree of universality into the project without losing a certain degree of particularity.* "

One problem which arises if you are actually trying to do something like this is introducing new writers. It takes patience, it takes a lot of indulgence. People do things wrong, you need to cover for one another, be willing to extend a hand until people come up to speed. Again, the question of credit is interesting in this regard. If you have a lot of writers credited — and this goes back to the argument with the business affairs guy tearing his hair out about the money it's costing and we're giggling and saying 'Yeah, we're getting it all' — no-one on the show has cause for complaint. If you have to cover for the new guy, if his name is on the script but it turns out that when the script is done not one word of his is in it, the three people who've been around a long time, who've wound up doing it all can hardly complain because over a number of scripts everybody is getting plenty of credit, more than they deserve. It's a strong incentive for people to work co-operatively.

If I only had one rule about team writing I think it would be to break down inhibition and encourage a co-operative spirit by whatever incentives are available — and I've mentioned a couple of the grossest ones. But also, you wouldn't want to have this multiple approach in the first episodes of anything when you're trying to sort out what the thing's about — in that case I think the first creators ought to be sure of their tone. They can't really pass it on to anyone else until then, and you can't be sure what it is until you see some of it coming back at you. So I would say that in the first portion of the first season this approach is not indicated at all. The second place where it's not indicated is the kind of show I mentioned, "**The Lonely Guy**", where you're only servicing one or two characters, so you don't need it. You're talking through the same guy, you're not trying to create the same kind of intense world. And then of course, thirdly, if you can't afford it. Don't do what you can't afford.

> " *If you're really building for the long term, there is some value in building a team.* "

The real alternative, depending on the stamina of individual people, is to write it all yourself. It's only 22 hours, it's only 22 times 60 pages, a year! That's an enormous amount of writing to keep fresh — I'm amazed that there are people who manage to do it. However, I don't think they do it to the concentrated level of this show; their shows tend to be a little less complicated. But that aside, there is the burn-out factor and if one hopes for a long-running series and one is dependent on only one or two writers and they've done all the scripts, all the material for the first season, the chances are, if not by the second then the third season, they'll have had it and they'll really want to be out of there. And then you'll have had it because you'll have nobody who can write the show. If you're really building for the long term, there is some value in building a team. As well as a political value: you're not dependent on one person who can get cranky and tell you to get lost. Even yourself.

WHAT IS COMMERCIAL: SEVEN APPROACHES

SIEGFRIED BRAUN

Head of Series Programming at ZDF, Siegfried Braun supervises "Diese Drombuschs", the highest rating series on German television, as well as being very active in the field of European co-productions. He is responsible for the recent hit series "Der Grosse Bellheim".

In *Adventures in the Screen Trade*, William Goldman makes the statement, "Nobody knows anything." And that's exactly how many executives, commissioning editors and producers feel in this business, when they try to figure out what is commercial. Everyone would produce nothing but hits if they could. Nobody has an infallible touch, but some producers are more consistent than others.

Unfortunately, since no one is sure what makes a script or programme commercial, there is often an unwillingness to think about commercial elements at all.

With the help of experts like Michael Hauge and Linda Seger, I have tried to identify what makes a script commercial. What are the criteria that producers in studios and commissioning editors in TV stations use in evaluating scripts or ideas presented to them? There are seven questions that can be considered to test the commercial values of a project. You may find them very basic and self-evident, but I get several hundred scripts every year and most of them do not answer even a few of these questions positively.

FIRST QUESTION: DOES IT HAVE A HOOK?

A hook is that aspect of the story that allows it to be quickly and interestingly summarised in one or two lines. Such stories are also often referred to in the industry as being "high concept". "**Back to the Future**" had a strong hook: a young man travels back in time, where his mother falls in love with him. "**Tootsie**" had a strong hook: an unsuccessful actor suddenly becomes a huge success, when he's pretending to be a woman. There was a strong hook for "**ET**": a young boy has to save a friendly alien from the humans who hunt him. "**The Gentlemen Players**", a ZDF drama series, has a strong hook: will four old, retired men be able to demonstrate their superiority to the yuppies and save the department store they used to run before they retired?

> " *No one is sure what makes a script or programme commercial.* "

Why the stress on stories with a strong hook? Mostly because if you can get people interested in a film or TV programme with one or two sentences, you have the makings of a terrific ad campaign. In cinema and TV ads, there is only room for a picture and a line or two. If you can use these ads to lure people into the theatre or to the TV set, they will in turn spread the word.

There are various types of hooks.

One is the main character. The story may be about a historical character in whom people are interested, such as Gandhi. Or it may be a fictional character who is already well-established in some other medium, as was the case with the James Bond books. Or it may be a new fictional character who is fresh and appealing, like Crocodile Dundee. Naturally, all movies and TV plays are ultimately about characters. If the character is to serve as a hook, there has to be something outstanding about him or her: the world's top spy with a license to kill, or a genial innocent from the outback of Australia who ends up in Manhattan.

Another hook is the situation that may dominate a story. For example, a man who decides to get revenge when his family is killed: that's "**Deathwish**". Or people stuck in a sinking ship: "**The**

Poseidon Adventure". Or a CIA officer who has to figure out who killed everyone in his section before the killer finds and kills him as well: "**Three Days of the Condor**".

Another hook is a social issue, such as wife battering in "**The Burning Bed**", or the rights of a father in a divorce case: "**Kramer vs. Kramer**". These types of stories are also particularly popular as subjects of television films. Even "**Kramer vs. Kramer**" might have ended up as a tele-film without Meryl Streep and Dustin Hoffman.

Yet another hook is to base the story on real events. People seem particularly drawn to behind-the-scenes facts relating to events they have read about or followed in the news. Sometimes feature films result, like "**All the President's Men**". But more often these stories end up as mini-series or MOWs: "**Poor Little Rich Girl**", for example, is one among countless others based on a true story.

> " *Why the stress on stories with a strong hook? Mostly because you have the makings of a terrific ad campaign.* "

Many stories are a combination of the above elements, for example, "**Beverly Hills Cop**" has a strong central character — a hip young black detective — and a strong situation, namely, the same detective being let loose in snobbish Beverly Hills. But often one element will predominate and that becomes the story's central hook.

SECOND QUESTION: IS THE STORY TOPICAL?

Again, it's not absolutely necessary that a story has this quality, but it helps. To be topical it need not have been ripped from yesterday's headlines. However, the subject should be timely in a general way. For example, "**She's Having a Baby**" dealt with yuppie concerns. ZDF is currently preparing a pilot which deals with the phenomenon of grown children returning home to live with their parents. The title is "**Hotel Mama**". Naturally what people are looking for in these programmes or films is entertainment, not documentaries about social issues. If your story can be about something already on people's minds, so much the better.

THIRD QUESTION: IS THE STORY FRESH?

When producers talk about creativity they usually mean, "Is it fresh? Is it original? Is it different? Are you grabbed by the premise?" Many of the most successful commercial films are based on an original premise that is well executed. There were no precedents for such films as "**Ghostbusters**", "**Wargames**" and "**ET**" and there have been no really successful copies.

FOURTH QUESTION: IS THE STORY ABOUT SOMETHING MEANINGFUL?

The best movies tend to have some sort of underlying message or moral or theme. Even when they are basically escapist. "**Tootsie**", for example, was about a man learning firsthand how people treat women, and changing because of that. When a picture is about something meaningful, that gives it a foundation, something upon which the story is built. The theme or moral doesn't have to be obvious. In fact, it shouldn't be obvious or the film may seem heavy-handed or propagandist. When it is well done, the majority of an audience will probably never stop to think about it, but it will be there and it will have served you, as the writer, as a central, if hidden, aspect of your story.

FIFTH QUESTION: DO YOU HAVE A GOOD CONFLICT?

Most successful movies are about a central character who wants something, or someone trying to stop this character from getting it. You should be able to identify easily what it is your main character wants. It could be to track down a killer, to return home before someone dies, to help an alien get back home, to steal the crown jewels, to win the woman of the character's dreams, or to save a firm in jeopardy.

You should be able to state who or what is opposing your main character. It could be the police, the daughter-in-law, Interpol, the parents of the woman of the main character's dreams, or the yuppies who don't like retired directors interfering in their business.

The match between your protagonist and your antagonist has to be an even one if the story is going to stay interesting. After all, the most exciting sports events are the ones that aren't decided until the final moments. If one team has a huge lead at half time, we tend to lose interest. In many movies or series episodes, it's a foregone conclusion that the hero will win. It seems unlikely that James Bond will ever be defeated by the forces of evil. Nonetheless, the writers keep trying to come up with more and more villains and opponents for him, so that we can at least believe for a while that this time it might just be the bad guy that does him in.

Your protagonist can be an underdog but if he is, he has to have certain skills or advantages that compensate for the other side's superior strength. This can go from the sublime to the ridiculous. In "**Rambo**" one man takes on an army and wins, but Rambo is an American and one who is not only mad as hell but also muscular, and the others are only skinny foreigners. In its own comic book terms it worked.

> " *There is a big difference between liking someone and identifying with him or her.* "

SIXTH QUESTION: DOES YOUR STORY HAVE A CLEAR-CUT AND POSITIVE ENDING?

For a while in the sixties there was a vogue for films that left everything unresolved at the end. That is no longer the case. Movie-goers seem to feel that if they have paid five or six bucks, they want an ending as well as a beginning and a middle. Furthermore, they seem to want happy endings, and most of the time what the audience wants, the audience gets. There are some stories that simply will not work with a happy ending. If yours is one and you believe in it, go ahead and write it. Just be aware that you will have a more difficult time selling it.

SEVENTH QUESTION: HAVE YOU DONE A GOOD JOB ON CHARACTERISATION?

There is a big difference between liking someone and identifying with him or her. Going back to Shakespeare, the Macbeths aren't exactly a fun couple we would like to have over for dinner, but we can see some elements of ourselves in them. While we presumably haven't killed for professional advancement, at least we can understand how tempting the grab for power can be; how poor judgement can take over in situations like that; how, having made a major mistake, it's impossible to go back and undo it, so you go on making mistakes. In more recent times, the characters in the "**Godfather**" movies are a pretty unsavoury bunch, but they have just enough humanity for us to identify with them on some level. More often, the protagonist is someone we do like and perhaps someone we would like to be.

So, can we establish a 'commercial check-list'? When you are first considering an idea you may want to take a few minutes to assess its saleability and question whether it is commercial or not. Here are the main questions in check-list form.

1 - Does the idea have a strong hook? See if you can state it in a sentence or two.

2 - Is the idea topical? If so, how?

3 - Is the idea fresh?

4 - Does the story have a basic theme or moral? What is it?

5 - Does the protagonist have a strong goal? What is it?

6- Who or what is opposing the protagonist? How?
Is the conflict a strong one that can't easily be settled?

7- Are the protagonist and antagonist equally matched?
If the protagonist is an underdog, what are the forces that help him or her match up to the opponent?

8 - Is there a clear resolution of the story? Is there a happy ending?

9 - Will the audience be able to identify with the protagonist on some level? Have you avoided the use of offensive stereotypes?

10 - Can you state what it is about this story that makes you believe it's worth telling, and that will make people pay real money to see it, and spend one and a half hours of their time in a movie theatre or in front of their TV set?

You can analyse the saleability of an idea before you have worked it out in detail. Before you write it, give careful consideration to its structure and to the characters. Ultimately, its commerciality has much to do with your own "connections" to the project. If you feel passionately about the story, if you have some personal involvement with the subject matter and characters, then you have made a start in finding what's "commercial" for yourself.

In the final analysis, executives often say, "It's all subjective". And they are probably correct. It all begins with our personal connection to the story, with being able to communicate the feelings and excitement which make us want to share a special story with millions of other viewers.

TIGHTROPEWALKING: THE SCRIPT EDITOR

LILIE FERRARI

Lilie Ferrari worked on the top rating BBC series "EastEnders" and is now writing episodes for various TV series as well as feature film scripts and novels.

In many European countries programmes are apparently produced without a script editor. My aim is to persuade you that not only does your project need a script editor, it cannot achieve optimum success without one; and I'm addressing you from the point of view of a writer now, not a script editor.

As a writer, the script editor is my friend, my ally, my resident expert, a shoulder to cry on, a mother figure to whinge at, and a complete bastard if things go wrong. This figure is essential in my life as a writer. And I want to persuade you that the script editor should be an essential part of your production.

How do you become a good script editor? There are no schools or classes for script editors, as there are for directors, writers and actors. However, it is generally accepted that being a good script editor is about an ability to communicate, an ability to get on with some often extremely difficult people, and about having a huge level of energy and commitment to the project being worked on. You can't be trained to have these qualities, you're born with them. But you *can* learn how to structure a script and make it work, and it's a matter of some annoyance and frustration to me that the broadcasting institutions and film schools in the UK don't recognise this by offering formal training. The usual way to acquire the skills of a script editor is to be thrown in at the deep end and just start the job. Can you imagine what an uproar there would be if directors and actors did the same?

Before becoming a full-time writer, I worked as a script editor on one of the UK's most successful long-running serials, the BBC's "EastEnders". "EastEnders" is transmitted twice weekly in the UK, runs for approximately 28 minutes, and is scheduled on Tuesday and Thursday evenings at 7.30, which is considered the prime-time soap slot. Its biggest rival "**Coronation Street**" is transmitted on Mondays, Wednesdays and Fridays, also at 7.30. "EastEnders" average audience ranges from 20 million in winter to about 14 million in summer, when people watch less TV. It usually competes for the number one spot in the viewing figures with "Coronation Street".

> " *The usual way to acquire the skills of a script editor is to be thrown in at the deep end and just start the job.* "

I'm sure you all know why soaps are so popular with broadcasters. They're very cheap television. An average "EastEnders" episode costs approximately £82,000 to make in above-the-line costs. An episode of something like "**Spender**" (a 50' weekly run-of-the-mill police drama) costs £3-400,000, and a "Screen Two" (a feature-length one-off drama) costs about £700,000. However, even though soaps are cheap drama, in the UK you won't find producers skimping on script editors — they usually have several.

I was a script editor on "**EastEnders**" for eighteen months, which is a long time on a soap opera. Working on a soap opera in the UK is a bit like being sent to the salt mines — it's perceived by everyone else in the television industry as the most heinous form of punishment. Imagine the speed at which things are done when working on a drama series — say a thirteen-parter. Now triple it. Now triple it again. That's about the pace of a script editor's life on a soap opera. You are working on fifty-two hours of drama in a year, one hour's drama a week, that's two thirty-minute scripts every seven days, and that way insanity lies. The biggest strain on a script editor working on a soap is the lack of time. There's a maximum of four months between commissioning the first draft of a script to the date of transmission, often less; and the transmission dates are set in concrete. There's no chance of delaying production if things go wrong. But although it's accelerated, the work of a script editor on a soap is only marginally different from that of a script editor on a long-running series, so I hope I can explain the workings of both.

Having said that there is no formal training for script editors, I want to acknowledge the work of several BBC script editors who have produced sets of notes to pass on to their successors, some of which I have quoted in what follows.

SO WHAT IS A SCRIPT EDITOR?

> " *The script editor is there to make sure the script works.* "

This is a bit like asking how long is a piece of string.

A general definition would be to describe the script editor as having a twofold responsibility — serving the writer and serving the organisation for which he/she works. The script editor is the vital link between the writer and the producer. Think about that. Think about what's uppermost in a writer's mind: writing the most exciting, memorable script ever written. And now think what's probably uppermost in the producer's mind: the budget. And the patsy sitting in between the creative act and the programme's bank balance is the script editor. Having said that, I need hardly tell you that most script editors are verging on the schizophrenic, usually suffer from extreme paranoia, and often burn out after a very short time and pursue alternative careers in the circus as lion-tamers or tightrope-walkers, since they have experience in both...

Obviously the duties of a script editor will vary, depending on the organisation for which he or she works. Working for a huge corporation like the BBC as I did is not the same as working on one intensive project for a small independent production company. But essentially the philosophy is the same: THE SCRIPT EDITOR IS THERE TO MAKE SURE THE SCRIPT WORKS. That's not to say there aren't dozens of other people who have the same intention, but none of the others is actually paid to do just that. The script is the script editor's total responsibility, and getting the final draft of a script as close to perfection as possible often involves starting work as far back as the original story idea.

The idea

The original idea may have come from an independent writer or may be the brainchild of people in your company. The script editor works with the producer and tries to decide if the idea will work. You may only be given one page of a general outline to start with, so you need to think of ways to tell if this idea will actually work on screen. David Crane, a BBC script editor, used what he called the "episode 7 test" — by episode 7 in any series the audience will have got to know the regular characters, they will know the set-up and they will know more or less what to expect. The script editor must ask him/herself whether the original story idea can generate enough material to sustain the series as far as episode 7 and beyond; in other words, "has the idea got legs?" If the whole thing is likely to grind to a halt by episode 4, it's the script editor's job to stand up and say so.

> " The script is the script editor's total responsibility. "

This is the first lesson in the life of a script editor — you must be prepared to look your producer in the face and disagree with his/her viewpoint. This is where the script editor develops lion-taming skills.

What kind of series?

There should be a clear understanding of what kind of series this idea will become. Early British drama series tended to be static, with self-contained stories and little character development ("**Dixon of Dock Green**", "**Dr Finlay's Casebook**" are examples). While series subject matter has changed little over the years (police series and medical series are as popular as ever), the structure is quite different now, and is constantly evolving. You will need to keep a constant eye on what is happening to series and serials within your own culture, and respond to changes.

These days in British television, for example, there is a far greater serial element in TV series. While each episode of a series may have a story or stories of the week, there is also development of characters and relationships as the series progresses. The audience can miss an episode and then come back to the series knowing they won't be lost, because they will only have missed the self-contained story of the week, and they will be able to pick up the serial story without too much difficulty.

Finally of course, there is the serial or soap opera, which has continuing story strands, developing characters and a cliffhanger at the end of each episode to draw the viewer into watching the next one. Episodes of soap opera very rarely have self-contained stories within a single episode, but this occasionally does happen (e.g. "EastEnders" occasional two-handers, where the programme looks at two characters in depth for thirty minutes and the "life" of the soap is temporarily halted). When a single-story episode occurs, it is usually done to indicate that something momentous is occurring.

> " *A serial is not the same as a series. Different rules apply, both in terms of narrative and character.* "

A serial is not the same as a series. Different rules apply, both in terms of narrative and character. It's as well to know which format you are going for, and to be clear about its parameters. A producer should already know this. A script editor's job is to make sure that everyone else, especially the writers, knows this too.

I have recently been talking to a very new young producer about an idea he has. It's a great idea. But the document he showed me didn't specify whether the idea would eventually become a series, or a serial. I asked him which it would be and he answered that "it didn't matter as long as it was good drama". I would beg to differ. You need to be very clear about what kind of programme you are producing, and why. If you are not sure whether all the stories have to end by episode 13 or continue for another year, how on earth will your writers know what — or how — to write? SO — A CLEAR FORMAT DOCUMENT IS NEEDED.

The format

It may be the script editor's job to devise the format of the programme with the producer. Certainly the script editor should be involved in discussions about the format *before* the writers are involved. Script editors and producers need to agree on basic principles, and producing a format document jointly is a good way of sorting that out. There's nothing worse than being in your first meeting with a writer, and hearing your producer say blithely "I saw this series as a kind of 'Twin Peaks' meets the 'The Cosby Show'", if you had been about to say that as long as the writer thinks along the lines of Ingmar Bergman while writing, he or she will be fine...

At "EastEnders" the format document was constantly being changed and updated as different producers and script editors came and went. But basically the contents were the same — the format document, currently called "Advice for Writers", tells writers about any limitations regarding filming — the amount of day and night shooting, the number of sets permitted per episode, the number of characters permitted.

The writers are also furnished with a complete biography of all the characters in the programme, diagrams of each of the sets, and a map of Albert Square, the exterior set of "EastEnders". When I was a script editor, they were also taken on a walk round the exterior lot, to familiarise them with the geography of the fictional world inhabited by the programme's characters.

Any specific research material relating to the writer's episode would be written up and given to the writer at the time of commissioning. It was the script editor's job to ensure that the research was carried out and recorded. If the writer had a story which involved a character getting advice from a lawyer, this would be researched — what the lawyer's advice would be, how it would be worded. Larger, ongoing stories might be approached differently. For example, when it was decided to run a major story about a central character being diagnosed as HIV+, all the regular writers were invited to talks by experts from AIDS organisations, as well as having discussions with people with HIV.

In a series, all this information would normally be incorporated into one document, containing the basic idea and theme of the series, when and where it is set, principal characters with biographies of each, filming limitations, and research material.

If the script editor is working on a series with serial content, it's quite likely that he/she will be given the task of supplying the complete breakdown of the serial background for all the episodes in a series, to be given to the writer. (For example, in the current series of BBC's "Casualty", the script editors passed the serial element — the ongoing story of the medical staff — on to the individual writers to slot into their episodes.) If this isn't done, there's a risk that the writers will stray away from the original scope of the series. e.g. in a hospital drama, there might be seperate stories every week of a medical nature; *but* the emotional ups and downs of regular characters would need to be charted by the script editors.

As the programme develops

"EastEnders" has been running for eight years. Most script editors work on the programme at most for two years. (I have known some who have lasted less than a week...) The same is true of the producers of the programme. This means that there is a vast bank of information about the programme that is not stored in any one individual's head. This is a valuable thing to remember. Never allow anyone, and that includes script editors, to keep knowledge about the programme exclusively in their head. They may leave tomorrow, and given the nature of the television industry, the parting may be acrimonious. At "EastEnders" we were fortunate to be able to employ a series of programme researcher/historians who kept records of fictional events on the programme and put them onto computer.

Most series don't have this luxury, and it's the script editor's job to produce a "bible" as the series progresses. This should note developments in characters and events as they occur. Each writer will bring something different to the programme, and other writers will need to be kept abreast of changes. If the series is working, characters will have gone on emotional journeys, relationships will have undergone change, events will have coloured characters' attitudes. Each phase of the programme's evolution needs to be communicated to your writers, or their scripts won't make sense. This "bible" is not the same as the document that many of you will have produced already, which is the initial outline of your programme.

Conclusion

So at this stage, for a long running serial, it's crucial that a script editor should be in agreement with his or her producer about what the programme will be like. The script editor will have collaborated with the producer to create working documents for the writer's use which will help the writer to write the best scripts possible. SO YOU HAVE YOUR WORKING DOCUMENTS TO START THE SERIES OR SERIAL. ALL YOU NEED NOW IS A WRITER.

THE WRITER

Hopefully, the script editor and the producer together will find some good writers. How do you choose your writers? And how do you avoid choosing the wrong writers? I can't answer that question, but between them a script editor and a producer must, because the working relationship with the writer is crucial to the script, so the right choice of writer is crucial to the programme.

On a programme like "**EastEnders**", there is constant pressure on the script editor from 'outside' to encourage new writers, and particularly to encourage writers from minority groups, who don't get much of a look-in in other forms of TV drama. This area is a real minefield. Should you, as a script editor, go for positive discrimination and actively seek out such writers? Or should you be sticking with the tried and trusted writers, whom some would call hacks, because you know they'll come up with a workable script?

The answer for our team lay somewhere in the middle. We tried to give time and attention to new writers, particularly minority writers, but we didn't positively discriminate in their favour, because we did not have the time to train them to write scripts. But we were also aware that the most experienced writer in the world can occasionally come up with a bad, unworkable script.

In my time as a script editor on "**EastEnders**", only one script was pulled, and that was a script written by a woman who has been writing for television for many years, and who has more experience than I'll ever have. But the script just didn't work. Even after several drafts, intensive conferences, endless phone calls, hours of nursing the writer and suggesting ways to improve the stories, the script was still a dud.

The decision to pull it was the producer's, and she nobly took on the task of breaking the news to the writer. At the time this was a great relief to me, but on reflection I wish I had been there with the producer and we had dealt with the writer together, because my relationship with that writer has been permanently damaged by the experience, and we never worked together again as script editor and writer.

I once went out on a limb and pushed for trying a new writer, fresh from the National Film School, who was keen to work on the programme, and whose graduation film I had liked. He assured me he watched "**EastEnders**" regularly, and was familiar with the characters. His training as a writer meant I could at least be sure he would understand structure and pace and would know how to write dialogue. I spent hours taking him through the practical workings of the programme, discussing the synopsis, working with him to find ways of making particular story strands work. I was fairly confident that he could produce a workable script; I couldn't have been more wrong. In his first draft, I hardly recognised the characters. Nobody spoke like a human being. It was as if Martians had invaded Albert Square, and had had lessons from Sir John Gielgud in how to talk Cockney. The stories veered wildly from the synopsis. Small incidents had been blown up into major dramas, while the main story strands had disappeared. Most of the episode seemed to be about a car breaking down, when in fact the central story as outlined in the synopsis was one of the main characters discovering who had committed a murder.

Through three drafts I talked to this writer for hours and hours — script meetings that would take a whole day — time you can ill afford on a soap opera. Each time the script came back in more of a mess than previously. Finally, as time ran out completely, I was forced to take the script home and rewrite chunks of it myself. I had to call the writer and tell him what I'd done, and ask him if he still wanted his name attached to the script. He was devastated. I'm sure I damaged his ability to write a script for a long time, and I have to take responsibility for that. I should have recognised that he wasn't ready for an "**EastEnders**" script, nor for the kinds of constraints a long-running serial imposes on writers. A soap opera is not the place to prove yourself as an individual and unusual new voice in television. I'm happy to say the writer has now fully recovered from his horrendous first experience as a TV writer, is writing happily for a long-running childrens' series, and is still speaking to me.

Another mistake potential writers make is to assume that soap operas are where you practise for the real thing — i.e. writing "proper" drama — a fifty minute series episode, or a ninety minute drama. I was once approached by an agent trying to sell me a new writer, who said "I think "**EastEnders**" would be a good place for this writer to cut his teeth, before he goes on to write for "**The Bill**" (a police drama)." That particular agent got a very terse letter back, pointing out that "**EastEnders**" was NOT a nursery for baby writers.

> " **Another mistake potential writers make is to assume that soap operas are where you practise for the real thing — i.e. writing "proper" drama.** "

I think the best advice I can offer on choosing a writer is that if at the initial meeting you have any misgivings about the writer's suitability for the job in hand, then be brave and say so. Rejecting writers is one of the hardest parts of the job, particularly when you have raised their expectations by asking to see them in the first place. But the quality of the script must be your first priority.

Once a writer is commissioned and working, the script editor's job is to make the writer FEEL GOOD about his or her work. There is nothing more debilitating for a writer than having a script pulled, or rewritten by someone else. I know that now, because I'm a writer myself, and have suffered the trauma of insensitive script editors and indecisive producers. So my advice is be definite about what you want from a writer, and if it looks like you're not going to get it, call a halt at once.

Anyway, let's assume that you have, miraculously, found what seems to be the right writer for the job. This is just the beginning. Now, for the script editor, the real difficulty begins: GETTING THE STORY FROM THE SYNOPSIS STAGE TO A WORKING SCRIPT.

That's the process I'm going to describe, using an episode of "EastEnders" to illustrate it. This process of getting the story from synopsis to script is hard enough. But what I'm also going to describe is something much more subtle and complex: GETTING THE STORY FROM SYNOPSIS TO SCRIPT WHILE MAINTAINING A POSITIVE RELATIONSHIP WITH THE WRITER.

This is very hard.

I am describing the system as it was when I was a script editor on the programme, two years ago. Whenever there is a change-over of personnel, particularly producers, then the system changes, as new producers try to prove to management that they can do it better than before. It's a human response to getting a demanding new job, but doesn't always mean that the new system is a better one. "EastEnders" has a new series producer, a new producer, and a completely new script department now, but since I believe the system that I worked to was, with a few reservations, a successful one, and it's the one I know best, that's the one I'm going to describe.

On "EastEnders", the writer was seen very much as part of the script team. There were two script teams, the Odd Team and the Even Team, so called because one team produced the two episodes that would be transmitted in the even weeks of the year (eg weeks 2,4,6 etc) and the Odd Team the odd weeks. The storyliner dealt with both teams, as did the researcher, whose job it was to keep records of the history of the programme, and to research the factual background to stories. Each team consisted of: story editor, script editor, and writer. The story editor was a script editor with a posh name and a larger salary, whose extra function was to oversee the smooth telling of stories and to suggest ideas to the storyliner. So, this team — story editor, script editor and writer, plus the storyliner and researcher — was responsible to the producer.

The producer (on "**EastEnders**" there was an 'odd producer' and an 'even producer') in turn was responsible to the Executive Producer, who in turn was answerable to the Head of Series and Serials in the BBC Drama Department, who had to report to the Controller of BBC1, who had to answer to the Director General, who reported to the BBC Board of Governors...

Very rarely did we get the feeling that anyone "up there" was interested in what we were doing, unless what appeared on the screen was going to be controversial and might affect viewers' willingness to pay the licence fee.

For example, an episode was written and shot which included a homosexual kiss. Discussions involved the producer with the Controller of BBC1, and after much argument, the kiss was cut. This kind of interference from on high is always distressing to script team and producer, particularly when it's about a controversial issue, because the producer and the script team will probably have had many moral debates before deciding to include it.

To return to the work of the script team, the storyliner was responsible for producing the story outline, or synopsis. This was usually done after informal discussion with the story editors and script editors and sometimes the producer, about the direction certain stories were taking. We had a very single-minded storyliner, so these initial discussions could be very fraught. His document would be taken to a weekly meeting, presided over by the executive producer, where we would either accept his document, perhaps only making minor continuity points (e.g. you've said here that this character quarrelled with his mother five years ago — in fact they made friends two years later); or there could be uproar, with huge and quite savage debates about stories and how to tell them. (For example, there was a proposed story in which the storyliner wanted a couple to make love for the first time shortly after the male character had hacked his way into the woman's room with a pickaxe. The women at the meeting objected strongly to the idea of depicting a violent act as in any way a turn-on for the woman character, and the story was changed.)

At this discussion stage the script team would already have made a decision about which writer to use, and the storyliner quite often tailored stories for particular writers with particular skills or areas of interest. For example, we had one writer who was an ex-market trader, so he was good at the mysteries of that particular world. We had another writer who was very strong on the older working class characters, but found it more difficult to write material for the middle-class characters. It was only sensible, given the pressure of time, to try and find stories for him that concentrated on his strengths, rather than his weaknesses.

In this weekly script meeting then, the script teams would come to a consensus (not always a happy one) about two episodes and how they would work, and the synopsis would now be adjusted to accommodate any changes decided upon at that meeting. This synopsis is what the writer was given prior to his or her commissioning meeting.

> " *A good script editor is able to glance at the producer's notes at the bottom of a scene, and interpret them in a way that the writer will accept.* "

The experienced writers would be commissioned to write both episodes to be transmitted in one week, which saved a lot of headaches in terms of continuity. The less-experienced writers were commissioned to write only one episode, with a different writer commissioned for the second episode.

After the script meetings and discussions the writer would then begin to write the script. Writers usually had two weeks to deliver the first draft.

The second draft would be due two weeks after delivery, and the "Director-ready" script would be due to be published two weeks after that, so there would be another two weeks if a third draft was needed. (This was unlikely with an experienced writer, but writers — even the most experienced — would often be asked to look at particular scenes again.)

With the arrival of each draft I would read and make notes on the script, the producer would do the same, as would the story editor. I would then meet with the writer and pass on the notes.

This was a very delicate business, and the hardest part of being a script editor.

A good script editor is able to glance at the producer's notes at the bottom of a scene, and interpret them in a way that the writer will accept. I have often had to convert one terse word like "nonsense" into a long and earnest discussion about the general dynamics of an episode and whether we are approaching this particular scene in the right way.

I will repeat, at the risk of boring you, that the script editor's job is to make the writer feel good about what he or she is doing. At the end of the script meeting, the writer should go away feeling excited about the changes he or she is going to make, and convinced that they will improve the script, not depressed and feeling that it's all such a mess it can't be put right — or, worse, that the changes that have been suggested are going to destroy the script.

> " *The script editor's job is to make the writer feel good about what he or she is doing.* "

The worst kind of script editor is the kind who says to a writer "Well, I don't agree with this note from the producer, but you'll just have to do it..." Where possible the script editor needs to hammer out a consensus with the producer about a script. Where there are slight deviations in viewpoint, the script editor must decide which way to go — with the producer's note or with his or her own note. But the writer MUST be clear about notes and what is required; and the script editor MUST be prepared to defend his or her own judgement to the producer.

Constraints for the writer

There are four major ones (in "**EastEnders**"):

I) TIME — for writing. The writer usually has only 2-3 weeks for the first draft, and possibly only days for other drafts. On a continuing serial the writer can't afford the luxury of writers' block; s/he MUST deliver on time.

II) TIME — in terms of the drama. The writer must include 10 minutes of drama set on the lot or on location, with the remaining 20 minutes set in the studio.

III) CAST — availability and numbers. The writer is permitted a maximum of 18 cast. Not all cast members are available every week; the actors have holidays, get sick, have permission to do pantomimes, etc. Writers have to juggle with odd, unexplained absences of characters in story terms when actors are not available.

IV) SETS — the writer is only allowed to use a limited number of sets, and must inherit two sets from the previous episode.

Now that the writer is equipped with the knowledge of what limitations are being imposed on him/her by the programme, s/he must also be aware of what has gone before in story terms, and must pick up on these ongoing narratives.

BASIC STRUCTURAL RULES OF ANY EPISODE

As a script editor, I had some quick basic ways of establishing for myself whether an episode was working. Briefly, they were:

1) Open with an exterior establishing shot
2) Get new story strands started early
3) Close down strands from previous episode
4) Pick up fast on existing states of play

Ideally, all this should be done within the first half of the episode! But having said that, all rules can be broken — and it would be a very dull serial indeed if every episode conformed to these rules. However, an audience will tend to read variations from the basic pattern as significant, so it's as well to think hard about whether deviations can be justified.

There is another rule of thumb that I applied in relation to each scene in an episode. It's a basic rule of drama, a question my producer asked all the time: "Does this scene move the story on?" If the answer is no, you should probably cut it. Given the amount of story material a soap has to cover in one episode, there is rarely room for the luxury of character examination, rumination or colourful illustration, unless these are drawn in at the same time as the story is told. So I always looked for each scene to have a "mini-catharsis", a movement forward, to keep the pace going.

Episodes should also reveal some elements that give the audience particular pleasure because they are predicated on audience familiarity with the genre of soap opera: references to the past and knowledge of character. Obviously writers who are familiar with the programme can give much more depth and colour to these aspects of a serial.

As with so many elements in the process, cutting scenes is a matter of painful negotiation. But everyone has the same aim (or should have!) — which is to produce the best possible drama in a very short time. The final product is a huge compromise, a struggle against time, budget, and for the script editor, the demands of other members of the production team. This requires enormous commitment and energy from everyone. It is not only the script editors who shape a script and ultimately a programme, although the script team has major involvement to the point where the script is DIRECTOR READY.

Between the Director Ready Script and the Camera Script, or Shooting Script, the script editor must accommodate the requirements of wardrobe, props, design, the actors, and the technical crew, all the time consulting with the producer and informing the writer of any changes.

However the aim is still that as far as possible, you want the writer to feel at the end of the process that he or she OWNS the script. There is nothing more demoralising for writers than to feel that a script has been taken away from them and changed into something they don't recognise, and worse, that they don't want to own. It's the script editor's job to make sure that doesn't happen.

Of course what THEN happens is another matter. The VT editor (hopefully under instructions from the producer) may well restructure your episode, and may well make further cuts — although a good tightly-timed script shouldn't need anything more than a trim here and there.

How the audience then receives the programme, and how the drama is interpreted, is also out of your reach. It's amazing how many moments get misinterpreted, and what audiences read into dialogue. I remember when we introduced Rachel, an educated middle-class character, into the series and had her gently reprimand another character for saying something negative about lesbians, the press and audience immediately decided that this character was obviously a lesbian herself, and sat back eagerly to await the first regular lesbian character in a British soap. They were disappointed.

I hope I have emphasised the team nature of producing a soap and in particular the importance of the relationship between script editor and writer. The script editor is there to do the job that the producer hasn't got the time to do — and that's to nurture the writer and make sure the final script is the best it can possibly be.

Obviously a good script is dependent on good stories, and soaps are voracious animals that eat up stories. There's an ongoing debate in "**EastEnders**" about where those stories should come from — specially employed storyliners or from the writers? But whatever the arguments, there is always a belief that the strength of the programme is in its writing, both in terms of storylines and scripts.

> " *The script editor is there to do the job that the producer hasn't got the time to do.* "

Without a good script, nothing works. And you are unlikely to have a good script if you haven't got a relationship of trust between writer and script editor.

I hope I've persuaded you that the script editor is an essential part of the process. And I hope that any new script editors out there are ready to give up their personal lives, read at least half a dozen scripts a day, edit another six, calm down a hysterical writer, soothe the fevered brow of their producer, and probably be very badly paid for their pains.

Learning the job of a script editor is about as pleasurable as going to the dentist. Once learned, carrying out the job can still be painful. Currently the only reward is occasionally seeing a strong script come to life on the screen and knowing that you enabled the writer to get it there. Until the day comes when broadcasters recognise the importance of script editors by investing in their training and development, and paying them the kinds of salaries they deserve, pride in your work may be your only real reward.

WRITING IN AMERICA

JOHN WELLS

Having produced several award-winning stage productions in the '80's, John Wells moved on to cinema and television, working on sitcom and drama writing and editing for ABC and CBS. He was a writer and producer for the critically acclaimed "China Beach", and wrote and executive produced the sitcom "Wild Oats" for CBS in Spring '93. He is Secretary-Treasurer and a member of the Writers Guild of America.

I think the difference between the TV industry and other industries employing writers in America, is that in TV the medium belongs to the writer. I think that this comes from the demands of series writing, the demand for turning out quality writing. We found out very early on that theatre tends to be controlled by the actor, film by the director, and TV, because it requires so many ongoing episodes, is a medium which has come to belong to the writer.

We didn't begin that way. It came out of necessity. If you talk about any American series you admire, there is a writer behind it who ran it. To give an idea of the ratios: there were three new shows on CBS last year which actually made it through 12 months, but there were over 75 scripts that were commissioned and written, 30 pilots produced, of which seven were actually put on the air. So we try a lot, which is the advantage of having the capital and size of the market that we have: we're able to accept a great deal of failure, but the successes are very successful.

In a trade paper this week, I read that "**Home Improvement**", which is a situation comedy, was the number one-rated show last week and was seen in 32 million homes. It takes 106 people to make it, so here you have a product that's used by 32 million people and is made by 106. That financial ratio of how many people are using that product isn't found in other industries, and consequently there's a tremendous amount of money that flows back into American television because of the size of the market, which means a lot of money available to be spent on development.

It is worth emphasizing that American television writers are required to work on a lot of things at once when they are in development, and through my talk it will become obvious why I say this. As an example, right now I'm writing a half-hour comedy series for CBS, a pilot we're going to shoot later this fall, and I have a one-hour drama for NBC, and a one-hour comedy-drama for ABC. I'm also supervising a one-hour drama pilot for one writer at NBC, and for another writer at Fox Television.

> " *American television writers are required to work on a lot of things at once when they are in development.* "

That is the standard number of shows that any writer may be involved with at any one time, in the hopes that one of those shows is going to go forward into episodic series.

When I say I'm supervising another writer, in American TV the networks are primarily interested in one thing. The one question they want to know the answer to, is "Who is the writer who is going to be running the show?" That is, we've come to believe that the success of a show is completely based on the individual writer who is responsible for that show. So anyone who has a track-record for being able to produce a TV show is asked to supervise other writers who don't have that experience yet, and it's almost impossible to sell a TV show that doesn't have a known writer attached to it, either writing it or supervising a less experienced writer. The network's question is always: who's going to run it? Because no matter how good that pilot is, what it really comes down to is who's going to be writing and supervising episodes 33, 34 and 35.

To give you an idea of how many projects writers in America stay involved in, since "**China Beach**" ended three years ago, I've written five pilot scripts, produced three pilots and only had one of those make it to the air. In that same period of time I've also been involved in probably 15 other projects, either as a supervisor or involved in writing in some way, such as rewriting other people's work. My point being that the writing process in America is not viewed in what has come to be known as film-*auteur* terms. By that, I mean that you can become very attached to what you're writing and really believe in it, but you're going to be required to be involved in so many other things at the same time, that it doesn't become a singular obsession. And, as I'll say later on, there are reasons why I think this is valuable.

As a case study of how many people get involved in an American TV show, I'd like to run you through what happened on "**China Beach**". It began as a half-hour idea: Bill Broyles had been a magazine editor, on *Newsweek*, and had also started a couple of regional magazines in America, and he was a Vietnam veteran. He had an idea for a half-hour comedy series about a touring girls' rock-band in Vietnam. Warner Bros Studios bought it, and brought in movies-of-the-week and feature writer John Sacret Young to talk about making it into a 2-hour comedy movie. They then made it as a 2-hour movie which wasn't actually funny once they put in dead bodies and whirling helicopters.

ABC liked it, they ordered six episodes, then after the sixth they ordered 17, and then finally, at the end of about a three-year process, they ordered a full season, which was 22 episodes. During that process there was input from the studio, Warner Bros, who purchased it in the first place, the development vice-president who was involved in it at Warner Bros, the president of Warner Bros, then it went to the network vice-president, then to the network president, then to audience testing, then to the programming departments at both the studio and the network.

At each one of these stages new scripts were written, so by the time it was put on the air there had been many rewrites of the show. And what I find remarkable is that it was a better show for that process. I think that, as writers, we tend to believe that the fewer hands that are involved, the closer it is to our own personal vision, the better the show is likely to be. I think that this wasn't the case in this situation because the writers involved knew what the show was supposed to be about. So all the additional input only broadened the appeal of the show, made the characters more interesting. Each new person who came in and gave his input had suggestions which allowed the show to appeal to even more people. And what I've discovered in looking back over the whole process, was that the original comedy idea was not nearly as interesting as the drama that emerged through this process.

Continuing on the theme of how many people get involved in an American television show, let me describe how staff-writing works, because that is really the heart of how most American shows are made, and I begin to realise that it is not a widely-used technique in European television. "**China Beach**" had a writing staff of seven to nine writers, who all had offices at the show and who were in those offices every day. Sometimes we worked as individuals, at other times it was team writing, where all of us would write one script together. Generally the daily schedule of the show began with an 8 am meeting with all the writers involved in the production discussing pre-production of forthcoming episodes, what we were shooting at the time, and the post-production schedule. From 9 to 12 o'clock we'd each have our individual writing times on whatever individual piece of writing we were working on. Then at midday we'd go to see that day's rushes of what had been shot the day before. Then from 1 to 6 pm we'd have lunch ordered in and work as a group. In my office I have white boards which cover all the walls and a large conference table in the middle. We placed the episodes for the year up on two of the boards, straight across. We have another board full of notes on individual characters that we'd like to try, and another board for the story-ideas. We started with that blank room and two researchers, and for the first month we spent all of our time simply putting up ideas, stories we'd like to do, character things we'd like to do, suggestions; we would bounce things off each other. No individual writer is allowed to come in and say "This is what I want to do and this is the only thing I'm interested in doing, I have this great idea". It goes up on the

> " "China Beach" had a writing staff of seven to nine writers, who all had offices at the show and who were in those offices every day. "

board and is communal work. Then we'll discuss the next idea, so that at the end of about two or three weeks, of everyone contributing, we look at what we have and pull out the ideas that we think are the strongest. Those are then put up on the boards for episodes, character work is put up, and we are then able to see where we think the characters are going and the shows are going, much in the way you would do a standard written bible. The difference is that everybody has worked on it and participated in it, so when the time comes to assigning stories to be written, everyone in the room has some awareness of and involvement in every story. So you might write a script but not rewrite it, as you need to go on to something else, and it can be rewritten by someone else in the room.

We spend a lot of time pitching stories to each other, trying them out for size, and once all the ideas are up on the board and we have a general idea of where the series is going and everyone is happy with the characters, then, and only then, do we start assigning stories to individual writers. Often what will happen is that a writer

> " *You might write a script but not rewrite it, as you need to go on to something else, and it can be rewritten by someone else in the room.* "

will say "It wasn't my idea, but I've become really attracted to this, I've been thinking about it a lot and I think I can do a good job", and that writer will then be assigned the story.

When the story is written it can be anything from four to ten pages long with act-breaks between scenes, very specific. It then comes back into the group where it is reviewed and everyone gives notes on that story. Again, you may or may not write the script depending on the pressures of keeping the show running, keeping the next episode coming up. Often you do a story only to have it assigned to another writer in the room. I know it sounds horrific, but you get a group of people together to pound out the problems and work through the difficulties. We bring writing problems back into the writing staff, so if you're having a lot of problems in a scene, you come back in and say "You remember that scene we all thought was a great idea, well, now I can't write it and it doesn't seem to be working". Somebody else may say they think they can write it and take just that the scene, and the next day they give it back to you, or everyone may see it as a problem and try to come up with other ideas on how to do it. The advantage of all this is that you don't have one single person responsible for doing all the writing, and I'm talking about 22 episodes, traditionally in America being shot on 7-working day schedules, so every 7 working days there has to be a new script, and that process continues for 10 months.

The production machine has to be fed, there has to be 7 to 10 pages of shootable material every day, and the best way to get that material every day is to have a number of writers who can write it. In other words, there are a number of people to whom you can say, "This scene isn't working, but I can't go to the set right now. You remember the scene, we talked about it, you go and do some rewriting on the set". It's not just me as executive producer on the show who's required to do everything every moment. As soon as that happens, the shows break down. There's an energy gained from team writing which I think goes counter to our egos as writers. Some of you might think that criticism and the collaborative process is going to reduce your ability to write because the criticism is going to be tough to take, it's going to set you back. But it is always the opposite for me. That criticism excites me, I get ideas from it, and when you're working with a group of eight to ten writers on a series, you feed off each other and there's a competitive spirit where everybody is trying to do a better job.

The disadvantage of being a producer and a writer on a TV series in America is the time-schedule. The typical working day for a writer on an episodic TV series begins at 8 am and finishes between 10 and midnight during the week, and then you're in on the weekends writing, because that's the only time you have when there aren't any production demands, and you use that as your writing time. You do that for ten months of the year, then you have two months off.

As I said at the beginning, the writer has become the person who is responsible for everything on an American TV show, and writers have taken that control because the thing that cannot be replaced in episodic television is the quality of the writing, which comes from your involvement in the entire process, and which I don't think can be separated from that process. My usual responsibilities are the scripts and the stories, communicating those scripts to the networks and the studios, but I'm also involved in the casting, involved and responsible for the budgeting, and for the money spent on each show. I work with the directors, I'm involved in the editing and all the final post-production, from mixing, to music and signing off on every reel as the final mix is completed.

At the same time I'm also responsible for daily communications with the networks and studios to let them know what we're doing. Now the reason for all that, I believe, is that the writer can't view himself as being separate from the total picture of the production. One thing I've found very helpful is having worked with producers early on and learnt how movies are made, how they're made financially. When I write something, I know how much it will cost, and so now as I write scripts I have an idea of what can and cannot be accomplished, so I don't write things that can't be done. I regularly write things which challenge the production staff and I try to spend every single dollar until somebody tells me to stop, not in a capricious way, but because I believe that our idea is to take every dollar that we have and to put it on the screen to give it as much production value — visual value — as possible.

All those things inform the writing process. If there are eight of us in a room coming up with stories and pounding out things that we can't afford to make, that's a waste of our time, and the only way that we have an awareness of whether we are wasting our time or not, is to have some knowledge of the production process itself. The collaborative process between writers, directors and producers can go in both directions, which is communicating what can and cannot be done, challenging each other.

Regarding the subject of collaboration between the producer and the network, in the American context, I have to say that I don't spend a great deal of time working on ideas before I've talked to networks, studios and production companies about what they want. I take a basic idea, an area I might be interested in, have a casual meeting with someone I know, a producer or network executive, and ask them if there is somebody who might be interested in this general area. Or ask them what they're interested in working on this year, and I get some feedback from them, and from that I develop ideas. Then when I go back in and pitch them an idea, it's already something that they've told me that they want to do, or that they have some inkling of. My point is, get some information before you go too far with your ideas. I used to think this involved sacrificing some of my artistic integrity but what I've found is that in incorporating ideas that are interesting to others, I usually end up writing what I wanted to in the first place, and the people I'm writing for feel it's what they wanted.

What the networks and studios work with mostly is fear, as they make lots of money and are afraid of losing it, and because of that fear they tend to gravitate towards 'franchises'. 'Franchise' means an area of proven story-value in the past. In America there are four franchises in dramatic television: there are doctors, cops, detectives and lawyers. So the franchise idea is very frustrating for writers, because you think all of these things have been done to death, but what the writer brings to it is an interesting and different angle on how we're going to look at something. If you look at "China Beach", it was sold as a medical show to ABC, as a hospital show set in Vietnam. But if you watch the series, you don't think of it as a hospital show, because there are so many other visual, character and dramatic elements.

> " In America there are four franchises in dramatic television: there are doctors, cops, detectives and lawyers. "

So if you go in and are working on a franchise you're solving a problem for the networks, as their biggest problem is knowing what the stories are going to be about. They may know you're a good writer, and therefore know that the first episode will be compelling and interesting, but what about episode 79? If the show you pitch has a limited franchise — for instance, journalism, because networks believe that subject is limited, and the stories each week will be very similar — you could say this person really acts as a detective, dropping buzzwords which make people happy. There is also a time-limit on pitching. You should reduce your pitch to 5 to 10 minutes. If you can't pitch it in a single sentence, and elaborate on the characters, the producer will say he can't get people to watch it. So the idea of having a franchise, a basic area which you can pitch and then latch on to very quickly, saves you a tremendous amount of time. You don't want to pitch something in a different world, so saying something's medical, detective, police, allows them to get the idea quickly. If you go to TV markets, where the stands exhibit their product, people are attracted to hooks: catchy high-concept statements, which will help you get out of the room quickly. The quicker you can leave the room, the less you've said to make them think of not buying it.

What is generally perceived as an American TV show? What makes it different? I think that there are simple and straightforward hooks by which people connect to American TV shows. Probably they are exactly the things that writers do not want to do, as though they are going to intrude on your creative process. However, I think it is actually useful in clarifying your creative process, while still allowing you to do all you want to do. So I am going to talk, briefly, about 'log-lines', act-breaks and visual strength.

> " *Conflict is what log-lines are about. A one-liner must have conflict in it, because your episode must have conflict.* "

A term you hear all the time is 'log-lines', which are one-liners, the same as pitches. Every episode has to have a one-line pitch. The term 'log-line' comes from the magazine "TV Guide", which gives the daily programming. The 'log-line' is the one sentence allowed for the network to describe each episode of the programme. And the network wants to know, when buying on-going series, what the 'log-line' is for each episode, because they believe that to a great extent people will choose to watch that programme based on how compelling that one-line pitch is.

Conflict is what log-lines are about. A one-liner must have conflict in it, because your episode must have conflict, whether dramatic or comedic, it's what stories are about. And it must be implicit in the one-liner. Something that becomes your responsibility as a writer is to know the needs of the people you're trying to sell to, and one of their needs is to be able to tell the story to everyone they work for, in one line.

The magic lies in selling your enthusiasm to the other person, and too many writers tend to sit back, not sure of how good their work is, having all the usual fears about the writing, but the buyers don't want to know about your fears. They want to know that if they buy it, you are so excited about it that you've got your word-processor in the car, and somebody else is going to drive you home, because you'll already be starting work on the first act!

For those of you who have to deal with act-breaks, I want to explain a little about this. There is a term used which is 'the button'. It means a little thing that happens at the end of the act-break to make sure people tune in again after the commercial. Like a minor cliffhanger, often without much script validity. Sometimes buttons are misleading, just to get people back after the break. They should be present in the story breakdowns, and it's important even when there isn't a need for act breaks, for example, in a film script, so that people don't stop turning the pages, whether they are directors, actors, whatever. Also, each character in an American TV series, whether comedic or dramatic, has stakes, or risks. There are always times when that character is at risk, when something is happening which implies danger, and will make audiences concerned for them. So there is always conflict or risk in characters in American series. The question is "What is at stake? Why are we here?". If in each scene something is at stake, the script propels itself more quickly.

> " Material that transports well is visual, you don't have to be listening to the dialogue to understand the story. "

Internationally successful American shows always involve risk — not necessarily a gun — it can be personal risk, risk of losing something in the family, risk of two characters fighting, risk of danger. Without risk, without buttons, we won't continue turning the pages. Our lives are ordinary, so why would people want to watch other people's ordinary lives? Audiences want to watch someone going through some emotional trauma. The problem for a writer is you get to episode 22 and think that the character has been through so much, is constantly at risk; but I find when I talk to people who watch the shows, that this isn't their impression, as they're not living with the characters every day, only one or two hours a week, and aren't thinking about them in between. They are not bored with it, and they want to be compelled by what they're viewing, although we as writers might be bored with the character we're living with 80 hours a week.

To finish, there is another very important element about American writing, which is its visual strength. Whereas I really admire European material, and can think that a script is extremely well written, I know a lot of international buyers won't buy it, because it is too literary. Saying something is too literary makes it sound as though I am suggesting removing the writing from our work. That's not what I mean. The material that transports well is visual, you don't have to be listening to the dialogue to understand the story. It's the basic visual images that tell the story. We used to have an exercise on "**China Beach**" which may seem arbitrary but will probably work on your scripts: remove every third line. There is probably too much dialogue in any script you write, because as writers we are too interested in words. Words belong to the theatre, where you can't see the play visually. The characters tell the story, and you should be able to understand it with the sound turned down.

> *" There is probably too much dialogue in any script you write, because as writers we are too interested in words. "*

In fact, I think that usually the dialogue should not refer to the scene in action. The only way we know what the scene is about is due to the way the writer has set up the dramatic situation, letting us know that there is conflict in where they've met, why they're there. These are the things that tell the story. So you give the director and actors the story in the way the scene is set up, so that dialogue is almost counter to what is being said. The more story-telling you do, the more you ask yourself how to do a certain scene with less dialogue — how to add to it visually — that sort of symbolism and the use of other situations is what propels the story, and fits into what we see as being American television. That allows American writers the freedom to pull back on having to describe the characters with too many words.

I hope that I have managed to outline the position of writers in American TV, and to give you an idea of their importance in the industry.

WRITING IN EUROPE

GUY MEREDITH

Guy Meredith has been a full-time writer for fifteen years and has written many episodes for television series and also the scripts for two films, "Jazzman", and "El Hombre de la Nevera".

The first impetus for PILOTS was: why don't our European programmes travel, why don't they cross borders, make sales to other countries, even within the same continent? The obvious answer was they're not good enough. Maybe that's a bit pat but there is certainly some truth in it. After all, no programme is ever good enough — "No work of art is ever finished, only abandoned," as somebody said.

But the point was, we did have a yardstick to measure *why* they weren't good enough. We had the American yardstick, American programmes to measure ours against. If a European programme sells to ten countries, it is considered quite of a success, whereas an American programme could sell to 50 countries without being a great talking point around the pools of Los Angeles. The question was, how were we going to catch up? That's what really worried those who started PILOTS and others who, like me, climbed aboard quite early.

When you're talking about that gap between ourselves, as Europeans, and the United States, there are of course factors which have nothing to do with the quality of writing or production that make American programmes more saleable. One is the language — the English language. A significant number of countries in the televisual world either have English as a first language or, more particularly, as a second language which a good proportion of the population speak well enough for sub-titled programmes to be used as a free English lesson.

But cultural reference is probably more important. The Americans have exported their culture — their non-television culture — in advance. We all live in what are, to an extent, commercial provinces of America. We all know what Levis and Big Macs and Coca Cola are and, importantly, we know that they are something more than mere clothing, food and drink, that they have something to do with a certain lifestyle. And when they figure, or that lifestyle figures, in American programmes we know immediately where we are and we feel at home. This contributes considerably to the success of American programmes abroad.

> " **"No work of art is ever finished, only abandoned,"** as somebody said. "

But, having said that, we can't simply sit back and give up. There is an American style of writing, which our American guests and others have touched on during the PILOTS workshops. This particular American style is very saleable across the globe, it has a very widespread appeal. I want to pin this down and see how it relates to us as Europeans. And I hope to do that by showing four sets of programme clips, two to a set, one American, one European, and comparing them. Each set is a different category and I've called them: action, emotion, sex and violence.

First we will look at action. What I want to show you is a clip from the new Steve Bochco production "**NYPD Blues**" and one from the British police series "**Between the Lines**".

Now "**NYPD Blues**" moves incredibly fast. This is the first episode of the series and the protagonists are two cops, Sipowitz and Kelly. It's really impressive when you watch the opening of this show against the clock to see how they get it off the ground. They establish that Sipowitz's job is in danger in about the first 30 seconds and then the characters of the two cops take about another minute and a half to outline in a confrontation scene between the two of them. Then you find that Kelly's left his wife, or she's left him, and that's the cross his character has to bear. This is the very first episode of the series, remember, and everything necessary has been set up within four minutes.

I think, by comparison, "**Between the Lines**" does look a bit ponderous. I don't think there's anything wrong with the show — just, by comparison, it looks slower. It's often been said that there's too much talk in European drama but I don't think that's true. In "**NYPD Blues**", as in "**Hill Street Blues**" and a lot of other shows, they're talking all the time. It's what they're talking *about*, of course, that's important. There is a tendency to give information in European drama. We saw a little of it in "**Between the Lines**". There was an exchange between the two policeman which went, "I have to tell you there's going to be grief if the wheel comes off this one." That's slang for "There's going to be trouble if anything goes wrong." It's rather heavy-handed.

> " *There's television reality and there's everyday reality.* "

Apart from the question of pace there is also the question of realism. I think what these shows demonstrate is two different sorts of realism. I'm prepared to believe when I look at "**NYPD Blues**" that this is exactly what New York is like — tough, gritty, fast-moving, violent. The reason I'm prepared to believe it is that I see New York and America all the time in television drama and my actual knowledge of New York doesn't matter at all. On the other hand, I've lived in London most of my life and I recognise it completely when I see it in "**Between the Lines**". I also recognise that the job of the police is for the most part rather plodding and systematic. And the British drama is based on that, but making the most of it.

So there's television reality and there's everyday reality. America *can't* be as violent as it's portrayed, there wouldn't be anyone left, but both we and the American viewing public are prepared to lap up the dramatic representation. In Europe we need to establish a link with what's going on outside our windows and, though we naturally spice it up, we can't afford to stretch that link too far.

To examine emotion, I want to show you two film clips, one from "**Scent of a Woman**", the other from Bertolucci's "**The Conformist**". There's a blindness theme that runs through them both and that's why I've chosen them. Now, in "**Scent of a Woman**", we're looking at the scene where Al Pacino is going to commit suicide, to shoot himself. And the kid's trying to stop him. It's a five minute scene or so and you can run through the emotions that are coming off the screen, one after another. My list goes: despair, fear, anxiety, affection, self-pity, pity, bitterness, anger, courage, determination. And pathos, interestingly, in the music. You can't ask for much more than that in five minutes. Or can you?

In "**The Conformist**", in the scene where Trintignant confronts his blind mentor at the party, you get those same emotions but they're much more oblique. Just to give a couple of examples: pity, instead of coming from the sighted man to the blind one, travels the other way round. The blind man feels that Trintignant, the "conformist", is not normal and his heart goes out to him. Here, Trintignant is the one who's full of self-pity. And pathos, when the blind man says, "A normal man is one who turns to look at a woman's backside". That's pathetic in the best sense because obviously it's something he can't do. And we get anger and fear and all sorts of other things in that horribly comic and tragic fight scene between two blind men. Beneath which, interestingly, the music is resolutely cheerful, in counterpoint.

> " Americans are bolder — or more shameless, depending how you want to look at it — about hitting emotions on the nose. "

What do we learn from this? That Americans are bolder — or more shameless, depending how you want to look at it — about hitting emotions on the nose. And that, without doubt, accounts for the viewability of American products worldwide. Some hot dialogue will go in which will arouse your own emotions very quickly, if you're prepared to go with it. And we do go with it because they are Americans being portrayed. If they were Europeans acting in such an up-front way it might look very odd because we — not all of us, of course, but many of us — have a tendency to hide our emotions.

So that puts us, as writers, in an even bigger bind. Because we're not trying to make art movies like Bertolucci, we're trying to make popular series. And yet, given that we're tied in to some form of everyday reality — what we see through our windows — we simply can't make our scripts as overtly emotional, otherwise every time the viewer switches on there's going to be someone very obviously in crisis.

Let's pause for a little sex. To start, we'll go back to "**NYPD Blues**". About two thirds of the way through the first episode we get a sex scene between Kelly and a policewoman. Apparently it caused a real fuss in America because there's a lot of nudity and a lot of movement. But at the same time it's shot in soft focus, slow motion, like a pop video, indeed with a pop song on the soundtrack. The whole tone of the show changes completely for a few minutes. Yet they get away with it, I think, because it's TV reality, because pop videos are something you see on your television, so you're into it and out of it and back with the story. There's also a high degree of wish-fulfillment. It's first time sex between these two and it's all absolutely beautiful, goes without a hitch.

> " *Let's pause for a little sex.* "

The second clip comes from the film "**Police**" by Maurice Pialat. I have to apologise for showing film clips but it's a problem getting continental series that are subtitled in English and I don't want to keep showing British TV. I think the lesson is the same anyhow. In this clip, Depardieu, a policeman, has brought a prostitute back to his flat. And he's nervous, really nervous, even with a prostitute, which he covers up by strutting around like a cock-of-the-walk. Which is not unusual for a man faced with a woman he hasn't been to bed with. There's nudity but no sex and in a way it's not about sex at all but about love and how difficult that is. You don't learn a lot about love by watching sex, but love is far more interesting, at least dramatically!

Just before we get into the final clips, let's try to address briefly the problems that are facing us. Our choice so far seems to be to write like Americans — hot dialogue, fast action — or to write about real people, real life as we know it. In fact, it's not that black and white. I worked on a series in Britain called "**Dempsey and Makepeace**", about a pair of detectives: she was a dazzling blonde, daughter of an English aristocrat, he was seconded from the New York police and carried a gun. Yes, it wasn't exactly realistic. But at the same time it worked, in a way. It didn't do badly in the ratings and it certainly sold throughout Europe. It was a sort of sub-American product and so we can do things that way, although I don't think we should.

It's not in anybody's interest that the world should become mono-cultural. Yet the more this sort of American writing spreads — whether it's actually written in America or elsewhere — the more we get on our screens, the less tolerance we, or rather our kids, will have for anything that's slower or more complicated, even though it is in some way a reflection of our everyday reality and emotions. The art of patience, the gratification that comes from building to something, will be lost. This is a real problem that PILOTS and the European industry generally has to face. But what weapons can we use to fight with?

> " *Our choice so far seems to be to write like Americans — hot dialogue, fast action — or to write about real people, real life as we know it.* "

Let's go on to the final pair of clips. The first is from "**Riviera**". Some of you will have seen "**Riviera**". Others will have been more fortunate — but all good things must come to an end. The reason I've put this in the violence category is that it does grievous bodily harm to the viewer. For those of you who don't know, the idea for this soap originated with an American company and they wanted to make it in Europe, for reasons I think of establishing a base here, maybe also for financial reasons. They eventually made it in France with a French production company, a French and American technical team and a mixture of French and American actors, the French having to dub themselves into English after the shoot. I'm not trying to be smug here but I think you'll agree it's a truly awful mess. It's not mono-cultural, it's not multi-cultural, it's just non-cultural.

So let's finish by going from the ridiculous to the sublime and having a look at a clip from "**Heimat**". It's the scene of Otto's death. Otto, you remember, was Maria's lover and an engineer who became a bomb-disposal expert during the war. In amongst a cast of wonderfully cherishable people — there were really no villains in "**Heimat**", only fools, and that's really significant because how many out-and-out baddies do we come across? — he was one of the most lovable.

And, if only because he was a bomb-disposal expert, we were pretty sure he was going to die.

It's the way he dies that's really significant, the way his death is handled. It's both comic and tragic at the same time, like the fight between the blind men in **"The Conformist"**, only much warmer. Otto and his sidekick are a sort of Laurel and Hardy duo, they make jokes — not macho jokes but casual everyday ones — and they're not exactly sure how big the bomb is but when the job's done they're going to treat themselves to some jam tarts. And then while Otto is working on the bomb, an old railway worker, looking like a sort of death figure, comes along and says, "I'm always on duty". But he's quite quirky, too, so it suggests that something terrible is going to happen without being pointedly symbolic. And eventually the bomb goes off and then there's a real masterstroke, comic and tragic in one shot, where the hats of the people watching all fly up in the air at once, just like in the comic books you used to read as a kid. It is likely that the director put that in, but if you were writing a script you could write it in to the screen directions.

I think what that clip shows us is what we ought to be trying for, what we're really good at in Europe when we're working at our best. That instead of playing what may be a very striking and showy tune with just one hand, we can play very disturbing harmonies with both, a counterpoint that will tug the audience both ways at once. So you're not moving faster but you're moving deeper. So that when the viewers switch on they may not be aware of a lot of things happening quickly one after the other, but of themes running concurrently. And, importantly, that those emotions or that emotional synthesis sets up a resonance in the viewer — not just an acceptance of what's happening on the screen and a mirroring of it, but a resonance which builds on the viewer's experience and turns the whole business of watching television into a far more rewarding occupation.

THE IMPORTANCE OF CHARACTERS

JÜRGEN WOLFF

Jürgen Wolff has written for many television series, including "Family Ties", "Gloria", "The Love Boat", and "Benson", television movies of the week, theatrical films, and award-winning short films. He is also the author of "Successful Sitcom Writing" and co-author of "Successful Scriptwriting" and "Top Secrets: Scriptwriting".

I want to talk about characters because they are the most important component of long-running series. This is a point that has already been made by Linda Seger and Adrian Hodges, and I think just about everybody that's had anything to say up here has mentioned the importance of developing fully rounded 3-dimensional characters in long-running series.

There's a difference between long-running series and films, because in films if you have a hot plot in a really active thriller or adventure movie, you can sometimes get away with paper-thin characters. A good example is "**Jurassic Park**". Basically the special effects have brought in an estimated $500 million around the world, so it shows how much you can do in a movie with relatively thin characters.

In television it's different because these characters are people we invite into our homes every week for half-an-hour or an hour. They have to be unique people that we like. They can be bigger than life, like "**Alf**", that furry creature from outer space who 'adopts' an American family. I don't think I'd want to live with

Alf, but it's quite fun watching him for half-an-hour every week. He's like some demented uncle who might move in with you. Of course, it's wonderful when the episodes are well-plotted, but what really sticks in people's mind is this furry, quite rude character who is like a child who never has to grow up. That's what makes him and the programme fun.

If we look at the classic sitcoms or one-hour shows, for example, "**I Love Lucy**", "**Bonanza**", "**Kojak**", "**Columbo**", these are all series for which we probably have a hard time remembering specific storylines. Maybe with Lucy we might remember the plots of a couple of the classic episodes, for instance, when she's working on a cake assembly line and can't keep up with it. But basically it's the character of Lucy that we remember and that we like.

> " *These characters are people we invite into our homes every week.* "

There was a wonderful demonstration of this fact a couple of weeks ago. Steven Spielberg's new series, which has been pre-sold around the world, is a very expensive action/adventure one-hour series, much of which takes place underwater. The first week it had tremendous ratings in the United States — the tune-in factor was incredible. Why? Because they had promoted it very well. Also because of Steven Spielberg. His name carries a lot of weight and people were curious. And so it was a huge success until the second week. But in the second week and third week it was beaten by "**Murder She Wrote**" — a series that is 8 or 9 years old now, which is hardly the stuff of great drama. Its plots are very much a formula. Some poor sucker dies every week within hailing distance of Jessica, an amateur detective, and every week the police arrest the wrong person, and then she figures out who it really is, and then everyone goes home, and the next week somebody else dies. But what's special about it is that it's about a nice character. Angela Lansbury plays it very well and she's like a favourite aunt who's smarter than she seems. People always underestimate her, although she's really quite bright; she seems a bit cool on the outside but has a good sense of humour; she doesn't really take herself as seriously as it seems at first. She's a pleasant person to spend an hour with, and it's enjoyable to see her get the better of the police and also of the killers. But when you look at a show that's been around that long beating all the accumulated might and money of the Spielberg show, you can take great heart in that, because as writers it's delightful that a programme which is character-based can make mincemeat out of one that's essentially a montage of special effects.

CINEMA VS. TELEVISION CHARACTERS

Obviously once you're writing for an established series that's been cast, you don't need to go into any detail about what the characters look like because they are already represented by specific actors. But it is particularly important in writing pilot scripts which are in effect "selling" scripts. William Goldman in his wonderful book *Adventures in the Screen Trade* makes a distinction between the "selling" script and the "shooting" script. He points out that you have to write these two differently. The selling script is designed to hook a reader, often somebody pretty low down the ladder of authority — a studio reader, or a reader who works for a network executive or for a producer. This person probably spends his

> " *Films are generally about people who change... TV series, on the other hand, are about people who don't change.* "

or her day reading many many scripts. Therefore yours has to stand out and the weakest area in the scripts that I've seen is usually in the description of character. You also want to have them reveal themselves through their dialogue and their action, but to hook that initial reader, to make them really see and hear what *you* see and hear, requires that you use some of the skills more traditionally associated with the short-story writer and the novelist.

Let us consider an important difference in characterisation in television versus cinema. Films are generally about people who change. We talk about the character arc — starting at a point, having a crisis and ending up somewhere else than where the character started. In some way the character must have grown or been affected by the action of the movie.

TV series, on the other hand, are about people who don't change. They are about people who may want to change, but who can't. I think in a sense this makes television series much more realistic. The entire economy of the United States is based on the notion that people want to change and never do. For example, consider all the diet books that sell every year. If people actually applied one of those formulas successfully there'd never be another best-seller diet book. But people try it and then it gets too hard and then they go back and they gain weight and they buy the next book.

TV characters are allowed to have revelations. They're allowed to learn a lesson — temporarily. I went to a weekend workshop a long time ago. It was a typical California weekend where you go and there's a counsellor in charge and you get to expose your deepest fears and anxieties to a group of strangers. There was a woman in it who talked about her relationship with men and she suddenly had a tremendous burst of energy and she said, "Oh, my God! Yes! Yes! My father! My father!" She talked about her childhood, the fact that her father had never really loved her and never accepted her and she said, "I'm going out with men, looking for the father image. And I find men that are so similar to my father that they reject me too! That's it!" I was quite impressed by this. It was a very dramatic realisation on her part. I was a little intimidated because I didn't have anything quite that deep to reveal. I said to her, "This is great." She was very blasé, so I asked, "Well, wasn't this a tremendous insight?" She said, "Well yes. But I've had it three times before."

In long-running series, particularly in comedy series, people learn the lesson but of course if they *really* learnt it your series would be finished. If Alf really learnt how to behave, what would the show be about? It'd be extremely boring. So Alf seems to learn a lesson and by the beginning of next week he's forgotten it. "**All in the Family**" is another one of the classic examples. It was based on the British programme "**Till Death Do Us Part**". Archie Bunker always learned at the end of the programme that black people or gay people or Hispanics, whoever he was particularly against that week, were OK after all. And then mysteriously in the intervening week he'd forget it. If he hadn't, what would the show be about? So we're talking, in series, about character revelation but not real change.

CREATING UNFORGETTABLE CHARACTERS: AN EXAMPLE

What we really want to do is to create unforgettable characters. One of the approaches is to come at characterisation from a different angle. Start with reference to your own life. There was in *Reader's Digest* magazine for many years a series called "The Most Unforgettable Character I Ever Met". People would write mini-essays about somebody they had encountered. It might have been a teacher, somebody in their family, somebody they met on the train, some-body who had made an indelible impression on them. It was always quite interesting to see who they came up with. So what I'd like to do here is to guide you through that as an exercise.

One of the good things about these kinds of exercises is that there's no right answer or wrong answer, so you can't fail at this. Think back and see who comes to mind when I say an unforgettable cha-racter. It doesn't have to be anybody you even know that well, although it can be. Just anybody that pops into your mind.

Some people see a mental image of the person, a visual image of that person's face or maybe an article of clothing. You may see them in repose, you may see them moving. You may notice things like the kind of shoes they wear or their posture or the way they move. Other people like to start with a sound — of a voice, perhaps the tempo of the way the person spoke, or that their voice was high or deep. And whatever your starting point is you can always use that to build up a more complete recollection of this person. Some people that we think of have a particular smell too, like a perfume, or pipe tobacco, or classroom chalk. And of course normally when we think of a per-son we get some sort of feeling associated with that person. It might be joy at remembering them, or a tinge of sadness perhaps, if they've gone. And if you're observing this person from a distance, perhaps you'd like to get closer. Of course if it's too close, you can always step back, mentally. I wonder whether this person in your imagina-tion has anything to say to you. Perhaps something you heard them say then, or maybe something new. I wonder if there's anything else that you remember about them that you haven't thought about for ages or that you didn't notice initially, but something that comes to mind now. Maybe even something a bit surprising. And then when you're ready you can mentally say goodbye to this image and bring back to full consciousness your memory if you choose to. Anybody find somebody that they are willing to say a few words about?

RUPPERT WIDDICOMBE: At school when I was young, we had a physics teacher who was an incredible character. He wore very typical English clothes. He was the sort of person who'd have arm-bands to hold the shirt sleeves up and he had corduroy trousers and brogues and you knew about these details because he used to walk around on the desks while he was lecturing. His physics, at a very basic level, has stayed with me. He was a great actor and his experiments would all be acted out with great passion. He was demonstrating pressure difference and blowing into a tube where a little coloured liquid would go up and he would huff and he would puff and he would try and get the liquid to rise. It would and I went after the lesson and tried that. I thought "I bet I can get it". And I fired the pink liquid right up to the ceiling. If someone interrupted him or was talking or stuck their hand up while he was talking, he would stop in mid word and he would just look at the person and when they put their hand down again, he would start from exactly the same syllable where he'd stopped. He had complete mind control over the people in the class. I have several friends who were at the same school, and we still talk about this man. Particularly about what happened to him later. There was a side to him which we never knew. He was always a very kind, interesting person but we found out last year or the year before that he was brutally murdered in his study at the school by a rent boy from King's Cross. He exists in a dual state as far as I'm concerned. This man that I knew when I was a 14-year-old and somebody I find out about from a tabloid newspaper, as having a completely different life.

JÜRGEN WOLFF: A very interesting character, colourful and easy to imagine from the specifics of that description, of how he moved and what he said; the tone of the voice and the interruptions. I formed a mental picture of the man, of what he was doing, how he walked on the desks and so on, very easily.

AUGUST GUDMUNSSON: I thought I should come next because my character is in some ways similar. Even before we closed our eyes I had thought of this man, and I haven't thought of him for years. He was my English teacher at grammar school. He was an extremely loud man. I later found out that life was simply too difficult for him but he was struggling all the time. He was very funny, full of life. He would, for example, come into the class and hand out Icelandic poetry and it wasn't his field. He wasn't supposed to say anything about Icelandic poetry. Still, he would hand this out and then he would read it out very loud as if it were extremely important for us to know it. In the end he committed suicide. He walked into the sea two years later.

JÜRGEN WOLFF: Some very dramatic endings to these stories so far. Is there one more?

SASKIA SUTTON: For some reason I hadn't thought about her for a few years but, maybe it's being in Spain, I suddenly thought of my flamenco teacher who looked exactly like the Queen. If you can imagine a Spanish version of the English Queen, who's very nasty, then you've got my flamenco teacher. She ruled her classroom and you didn't dare do anything wrong. You had to do exactly what you were told. Whenever anybody new came into the class and started chewing gum or talking to somebody, the rest of the class would all stand still, waiting for her to blow her top which meant we all ended up having a very painful hour. My family couldn't bear the idea that there was somebody in my life that terrorised me, somebody I was just too frightened of to deal with. They thought this was a very peculiar situation but I was actually too frightened to stop going to the classes. She was quite a character, and in the end I managed to have enough grown-up courage to stop being abused by her.

JÜRGEN WOLFF: Thank you. There are two reasons for doing that exercise. One is to start to introduce you to a technique that I find very useful — of visualization as a way to access characters. You use your intuitive and sub-conscious mind rather than only your conscious mind. And the other reason is that it usually, as it did here, brings forth some very clear and specific descriptions that allow us to see these characters quite clearly, and in some cases to hear them too, like the poetry teacher. For me that was primarily an auditory image, if I can use that combination, of hearing this man bellowing these poems at the top of his lungs, whereas with the other school teacher it was more a matter of the visual, of seeing him jumping around the desks. And with Saskia's teacher it was a combination because I was trying to think of the Queen of England but Spanish and cruel. That's an interesting one for your imagination to go to work on.

It's a good idea to look at the different components that we touched upon when I was doing the exercise with you, which are the visual, the auditory (what do the people sound like?), the kinaesthetic, dealing with how they move, and the olfactory (if there are any smells associated like perfume, tobacco, or body odour or whatever). Then think about what sort of emotions they tend to arouse in people as well as what their own emotions are. In other words, if you do all this you will start with a well-rounded notion of what this person is, and you can reveal these characteristics as you work through the script.

ANOTHER APPROACH TO CHARACTERISATION

I want to read two excerpts from a book which is called *The Agony and the Ego — The Art and Strategy of Fiction Writing Explored.* In the book, a British writer named Deborah Moggach talks about how she creates characters when she writes novels. She says, "More recently I was planning a novel about a man who had a lot of ex-wives. He sprang into life once I had pinpointed where he lived — one of those city blocks of mansion flats on the Edgeware Road. For days I sat in my car opposite the building and pictured him shuffling out — big, bearded, wearing espadrilles with the backs squashed down, and pulling along one of those matted little dogs that looks as if it has been run over. By this time his name had come to me — Russell Buffery. I knew he would shuffle along to the local pub because he was a boozer. I knew he would shuffle along to the chemist's because he was a hypochondriac and needed to buy Algepan for his heart and Fibergel for his bowels which were always giving him trouble. I followed him to the bottle bank. He was a late but enthusiastic convert to this and glared at people who threw green bottles into the clear container and clear bottles into the green until he became uncomfortably aware that wine dregs from his own bottles were trickling down his sleeve."

There is a very rich set of images here about this character, primarily visual.

And in the excerpt she says, "Once Russell Buffery was fixed in my mind I knew that one of his ex-wives would be a neurotic arty type who wore layers of clothes, sort of Miss Haversham meets the Incas, and who went to primal therapy groups. And that an earlier wife would be an ex-actress who ran an antique stall — one of those women with a sheepskin coat and a smoker's cough whose lipstick comes off on their front teeth. My hero collaborated with me on his own past, we discovered it together."

Again, this is an interesting different point of departure for finding the characters that you're dealing with — using the unconscious mind, in this case actually going to a place and letting the environment lead you into a character. Knowing intuitively that this is where he might live and saying "There's a pub. Would he go to that? There's a chemist's. Would he go to that? Why? There's a woman's dress shop. He probably wouldn't go into that. There's a hairdresser's. How often would he get his hair cut?" For people who get a little bit blocked on creating characters, I'm trying to offer some less traditional approaches. The traditional approach is to start with a list of characteristics and decide, sometimes rather arbitrarily, on age, college education, religion, etc. I often find that's rather sterile. So this is another way of going at it, and a lot more fun.

SECONDARY CHARACTERS

These techniques are useful not only for your main characters but also for your secondary characters. All your characters deserve to be real even if all they're doing is coming in and saying "Dinner is served". There's the old joke about the actor who's appearing as the grave-digger in Hamlet and somebody says, "This is one of the Shakespeare plays I haven't read. What is it about?" And he says, "Well, it's about this grave-digger". That's our view in real life, isn't it? I'm an extra in your movies. You're extras in my movie. To me my life is as important as yours and vice versa. And that's true of all the minor characters you have in your script.

There's a trap here — the David Lynch trap, I call it — of making everybody so damn quirky that they're all unbelievable and you think "What world do these people live in?" Every waiter is nasty. Every taxi driver is a Buddhist who used to be a Jew. I'm not saying go for the weirdest aspects that you can find, but find something that makes them individual because we all are.

Let me give an example from a script I wrote recently, where I've got two men in a park. One of them is sitting there feeding the pigeons and my main character, who's very depressed, sits down next to him. The man who's feeding the pigeons is an acquaintance whom he sees in the park whenever he walks through. My main character tells him what's wrong and the other guy tries to cheer him up. But it doesn't work very well. Finally the man hands him the bag of breadcrumbs and says, "Would you like to feed the pigeons for a while?" and he says, "No, I don't like pigeons." And the first man says, "No, neither do I". It's not a big joke, but it tells you something about this man's life. He's so lonely that even though he doesn't like pigeons, this is something to do, so he goes out and does it. I'm talking about small things, just to give a hint of characterisation to somebody who otherwise may too obviously be "the man your hero talks to".

THE ACTOR'S APPROACH

Finding and building a character really is, as you can see, somewhat similar to what an actor does when he or she approaches acting a character that's already been developed. I really recommend that the writers here, if you haven't done it already, take an acting class or an improvisation class. It's terrifying and you may be embarrassed but it's wonderful in terms of what you will learn as a writer.

EXPLORING RELATIONSHIPS

The other thing, of course, is to look at relationships — how people interact with each other. How does your character interact with other people in your greater cast of characters, how does he behave in general? One of the things that I find very useful when I'm starting to develop a character is to write some scenes that I know will never be in the movie or in the TV script. I just have to put a character into the world somehow. I start perhaps one morning, his alarm goes off and I write a few pages about what happens next. Or I put him in a pub and a fight breaks out. Is he the sort of person who would run? Would he get involved? What would he say? Who was he with? And so on. I did an interview with Alvin Sergeant, a wonderful writer who did the adaptations of "**Julia**" and "**Ordinary People**". He had this huge stack of papers on his desk. I asked him what they were and he said, "That's my next script." and I said "What is it?" It wasn't a ten-hour mini-series; apparently it was a feature script, despite being about 500 pages long. He told me, "That's how I get into my movies. I just start writing. Probably about a tenth of that stuff that I generate ends up in the script. Much of what is thrown away is the first hundred pages. Because at that point I don't know them yet — I don't know these characters yet. But I can't just sit there and make things up about them. I have to put them into action."

So that's again another approach if you find the traditional approach hasn't always worked well for you.

THE SUBCONSCIOUS MIND

There is one exercise that I do in some workshops, which I won't do here because it's more appropriate when it's *all* writers. But I'll give it to you as an example of the kind of thing you can do on your own. There was a group in a workshop that was working with television scripts, where they had a main character in mind and I had them do a visualisation of their character. And then, not only did they see the character, the way you were imagining the person that you were remembering, but I then had them imagine that character turning their back to them and standing there. And then they actually in their imagination step forward into the body of the character and suddenly... it's wonderful to watch because I have them do this when they're standing up, and the posture changes and you can almost tell in some cases what kind of character they're thinking about without knowing who they're writing about.

What amazed me was the next thing we did, an exercise I had never tried before where I said, "OK, you, as this character that you're writing about, think back to an important birthday that you can remember, sometime in your life." It's the birthday of the character, not the writer. And frankly, I had no idea whether this would work but I thought it would be fun to experiment with them. I led them through this exercise with "What happened? What did you see? What did you hear? What did you feel? Who else was there?" etc. And then they all sat back down. There were about 25 people or so, and I polled them one by one. I thought, "I hope a few of these people were able to do this." Every single person came up with *amazing* things that most of them were surprised to have discovered because they hadn't consciously thought, for example, about this character's tenth birthday which was the birthday that she overheard her parents arguing and realised she was never wanted as a child. It was always a birthday of some significance. Almost all the writers were amazed at how much of a revelation this was to them about their own characters.

> " *Our biggest quest is trying to get to the point where we get to know our characters as well as we do the people in our lives.* "

I have a solid belief in the ability of our own subconscious minds — it's way ahead of us. Whatever you're writing today, your subconscious mind is a few miles ahead waiting for you to catch up. It's important to open yourself up to that fact and to take advantage of that as a tool.

What I've really been talking about is how to use approaches which allow you to *discover* the characters rather than to build them. We've come full circle I think, back to the point that what matters most in our lives and also in our fiction, whether it's comedy or drama, is other people. Our biggest quest is trying to get to the point where we get to know our characters as well as we do the people in our lives. That's when they start to talk, that's when they come up with ideas of their own, that's when they make our job easier, and sometimes more difficult, because they don't want to do what we thought they should be doing. That's when the real world of writing comes alive and the end product is a script that also comes alive.

CONFLICT AND CONTRAST IN SERIES TELEVISION

LINDA SEGER

*Dr. Seger began her script-consulting business in 1983 and has given seminars
for ABC, CBS, Embassy Television, as well as producers and writers
in Canada, Italy, Britain, Australia and New Zealand.
Author of several successful books on scriptwriting.*

How do you create a series that has the potential to run for ten years?

When I thought about this, I realised there were two concepts that are extremely helpful for putting into your bible that can make the difference between a short-running series and a long-running series. The two concepts are the concept of conflict and the concept of contrast. I want to talk about them separately, and you'll see then how they actually go together.

One of the best ways to define conflict is when two people want mutually exclusive goals at the same time. One person's going to win and one person's going to lose. Conflict is really the lifeblood of drama. Conflict on many levels seems to be what drama's about.

Generally, in most American movies, the kind of conflict you see is the conflict of action. It means that people wound and kill and maim and chase and explode. It's what they call the punchy kind of conflict. On the one hand this is very strong conflict — it's very direct, it's very exciting and this is one of the reasons why a lot of very bad American movies do so well all over the world. Because it's very dramatic, it's easy to understand, and you don't have to have great dialogue to do it. The problem, of course, with this kind of conflict is that it becomes very one-dimensional and one-note and pretty soon it's just another car chase, just another murder, another shooting, another explosion and nothing else is being done with it and it wears thin very quickly.

Action is often the key to drama, but that action can be so much more than simply this kind of American punchy action. One of the ways to define action is to say that it's an event or it's what people do and that if you were to turn off the volume of your television set you would still know what's going on because action or the particular events are carrying the story.

> **" Conflict is when two people want mutually exclusive goals at the same time. "**

When you are writing about action, try whenever possible to show what is going on as opposed to talking about it. For instance, if you were going to have somebody turned down for a promotion, you can do that scene in dialogue. Somebody comes in and says "Well, we decided to pass you over and to give your job to somebody else." But there are ways to visualise that conflict or action, whether it's by showing the person's name being taken off the door, or by them being handed a pink slip — both of which are very different from saying "You're fired". Yet they have the same, or greater, effect. So action can be used as a basis for all your stories.

The wonderful thing about working with action is that it is always part of a sequence of events, and as soon as you have a sequence of events you begin to have development and development is one of the important elements you're always looking for. To paraphrase Aristotle, "sequence of events, relationship of events and development of events is 'good', episodes by themselves is 'bad'".

So, when you are thinking of action you are also getting more drama, because you are also dealing with reaction. For every action there is usually somebody responding. Now, in American films somebody shoots someone so the next person has to go and shoot them in revenge. Actually in a many Greek plays you have that same idea — somebody kills someone, then they have to kill the mother, and then they have to come back and kill the father, so you have all this reaction going on.

The problem you reach with conflict of action is not only that it becomes repetitive, but that it becomes one-note and many times certain actions never resolve things. So, one thing to begin to think about is not just conflict of action but conflict of attitude.

Conflict of attitude can be extremely useful to writers because, if you think about it, a lot of European television relies more on character and more on psychology than much of what you see on American television. This is a way for you to keep real drama and real conflict within your work while making it European instead of American.

> " *Conflict of attitude has to do with how characters think.* "

The way to think about it is to remember that when you talk about dimensional characters, these characters think, act and feel. Conflict of attitude has to do with how characters think. When you create your characters, you are probably thinking of three different levels to your character: philosophy, concern and values. They all define conflict of attitudes. One is the level of philosophy — what do your characters believe? Are they religious or not religious? What are their politics? What are their beliefs on certain issues? What is their philosophy towards life? And as writers and producers, when you think about the philosophy, this is something you want to put into the bible of your series but you probably don't want to put into your scripts because philosophy gets very wordy and having people sit around and talk about existentialism does not necessarily make good drama. But it informs your character and it helps you to know your character better.

Another way of dealing with how your character thinks, that is easier to do dramatically, is to think in terms of your character's values and your character's concerns. This is a lot easier to shade into a character and to show dramatically — the way somebody looks at somebody who does something they don't agree with, is a way of shading a character. This has to do with a conflict of concern and values. To give you a wonderful example, I'm sure most of you have seen the movie "**Witness**". There is a wonderful scene when John Book is showing Samuel the gun and Rachel comes in and Rachel's reaction, because of her value system, is immediate and very strong. When John says "Take the gun. Hide it." she takes the gun gingerly with her fingertips and carries it out. That's a very visual way of showing there is a conflict of value between her and John.

But a conflict can also be done in very small ways. When I interviewed Diane English from "**Murphy Brown**" for my book *Creating Unforgettable Characters,* Diane was telling me they were doing a scene between Murphy and Miles where they couldn't figure out how to shade the scene. It just was one of those very informational scenes and she said they couldn't make it interesting. Then they decided to give Miles a haircut and Murphy didn't like it. She spent the whole scene conveying this attitude to the haircut, which shaded the scene and made it very interesting.

People have conflicts of attitude towards all sorts of things, every level of what goes on. They don't like the tie the chauffeur is wearing. They don't like your bluejeans. They don't like the shoes you're wearing. They don't like what you're eating.

So working with attitudes not only gives you many ways to shade a character and to shade a scene, it also gives you an opportunity, in whatever kind of show you are doing, to deepen that show by simply presenting the attitudes of your characters. If you think about even the best cop shows on television, you often see levels of attitudes being played out where you feel that as you get to know the character, you get to know their stance on various issues and you're aware of them on a number different levels.

A character thinks, so there are philosophies, concerns, values, attitudes. Characters act, so there is conflict of action, and also conflict of decision, which is part of action. Many times in shows that are not very good the characters just act, they go out and they shoot someone. But the programme-makers forget that before the action itself, a decision must be made.

People often have inner conflicts over a decision. One part of me says, "I really would like to eat this", or "I'd really like to go this way", or "I'd really like to spend this money". But there's another side of me that says I really shouldn't. So, you can have the inner conflict over a decision or you can have the relational conflict between two people trying to decide what's the best decision to make. And again, these kinds of conflicts can be expressed in many different ways. Sometimes they're expressed in a joking manner, sometimes they're expressed through an argument or a confrontation, but always leading to a conflict becoming much more active — someone shoves, pushes, maims, wounds, shoots, explodes...

So we've discussed conflict of thinking and acting. The third type of conflict I'll talk about is the conflict of emotions. You can get a lot happening by thinking about the emotional palette of the character and how that emotional palette is different from one character to another. The first way of starting to think about this is by observing people in real life. People have different kinds of emotional palette. The Spanish are probably more emotional than, say, the Americans and that means that they will perhaps show a greater variety of emotions within a certain situation.

> " *We identify with people through how they feel.* "

A psychiatrist once said to me that we have four emotions — mad, sad, glad and scared. Sometimes people add the last emotion of hurt, and if you think of those five emotions, people differ greatly in how they express emotions and how they talk about emotions.

Remember, we identify with people through how they feel. When someone on screen feels, generally we feel. Now if the emotional palette of your character is very small, then what you might have to do is push that character into a situation that broadens the emotional palette. You can be sure that the most stoic of people, under certain circumstances, will feel emotional. What happens is that a movie creates a strong enough situation to broaden the emotional palette of the character, so we begin to see this other side of them, and can relate to it.

Let me give you a couple of examples from movies you might have seen. In "**Out of Africa**", Karen Blixen has one of the narrowest emotional palettes I have ever seen in a character. She responds emotionally to hardly anything, but there are a few times that she does. The first one is when she goes up for an airplane ride with Dennis Finch-Hatten. We all remember that wonderful airplane ride. And she is so moved by what happens, she makes this wonderful gesture: she puts her hand backwards, Dennis takes it and there are tears in her eyes. You think this moment is so emotional because even someone with that narrow emotional palette has been opened up.

Now the opposite. Tess McGill in "**Working Girl**" has a very broad emotional palette and you are constantly seeing her emotionality on screen. When she finds her boyfriend with another woman, not only does she get angry and you see it, she leaves and you feel her betrayal as she walks along the water and looks out over it. The purpose of this scene is to show her emotional reaction to that moment. Then, when she is betrayed by her boss, she carries with her the emotionality of the scene before, and the betrayal by her boss causes her to act.

> " *Characters don't have to talk about emotions to show them.* "

So emotionality can be part of an overall sequence which motivates action, which then motivates reaction. Or it can be a shading of character where two characters react in totally different ways; then you get a conflict from the way one character feels about how the other character is reacting. What comes out in this is a conflict of emotion.

Another thing to think about is all the subtleties of emotions. Sometimes in my work as a script consultant to writers, when I feel the emotional level of the script is lacking, I will tell them to go through the script and ask themselves what everybody is feeling in a certain scene. One way to do this is to recognise the different levels of emotions. So when someone says a character's mad — there can be anger, there's rage, there's irritability, there's being pissed off... there are all these different levels of being mad. There's glad from being ecstatically happy to being mildly amused by something. There's the sad, the deep depression to being a little down today, and scared can be everything from being totally terrified to saying "I'm a little nervous". So there are all of these levels within emotions.

In working on emotions with the character, remember that characters don't have to talk about emotions to show them. Find opportunities and ways for characters to show how they're feeling, rather than have them talk about how they're feeling. I think sometimes writers don't have quite enough trust in the actor's ability to show feeling and thoughts. I would recommend that you learn to trust the actor to be able to convey an emotion without having to talk so much about it.

The other side of conflict is to think in terms of contrast. Particularly in television series, it is not a matter of creating individual characters, it is creating characters in relationships that have enough dynamic to them; who have so much going on in their relationship that it lasts week after week, year after year, decade after decade. If you so choose, and the actors could stand it, you would have many, many levels of different emotions, stories, issues, crises, different relationships to play with.

Now what this means is that as you think about the characters that you create in your stories, you think in terms of the relationships amongst them as oppposed to simply creating an individual character. Therefore you think in terms of contrast, which is how you get conflict. And if contrast is written into the bible of your series, then you will always have conflict.

Contrast is often played as one-note. You know, if you take a show like "**Cheers**" you could say "Well, OK, Sam is the spontaneous playful kind of person and in the early years Diane was the more intellectual one." That show would have run out very, very quickly if that was the only note they were playing.

So, take your major characters, your protagonists, whether they are husband and wife, sisters and brothers, lovers, parents, children. Whoever the main characters are, you should begin to think of them in terms not of what they have in common, but what differentiates them. Try to be very conscious about this, because the more you think it through and do your homework at the pilot stage, the easier it will be as you continue with these series, because everything has been built in. The problem sometimes is that people get through the first six episodes or the first season and they literally have no place to go because there's not enough that has been built into the bible to work with. It is much more difficult to add it later on, because characters have already been defined.

One thing you might want to try doing is to make a chart. Take your two main characters and put down their philosophies. One character thinks this way, the other character thinks the other way. Then write down their attitudes to all sorts of things.

You can start by thinking about it in terms of physiology, that is, what do these people look like? Are they from different ethnic groups? Are they short, tall, fat, skinny? Are they blonde, brunette?

> " *The more you think it through and do your homework at the pilot stage, the easier it will be as you continue with these series, because everything has been built in.* "

But then begin to think of contrast in terms of smaller things. What do they eat? Is one a gourmet cook, while the other is a Macdonalds' person? Just that one idea with your characters gives you all sorts of situations where you can play the contrast through to conflict. The sandwich guy comes in and brings sandwiches. One guy won't touch them, the other one says "Oh, I love them and the more butter and mayonnaise you can put on it, all the better." Even if it's only there to shade a scene, you always have a dimension to make the scene extremely rich.

You can also work with your minor characters. For example, contrast your minor characters, such as two bodyguards, who might look quite different from each other, or a chauffeur who perhaps contrasts with the person he has to drive around. Think of all your characters in terms of ways that they can potentially contrast with other characters.

As you begin to think of contrast, you can then enrich the characters because you're going to start thinking more about what their motivation is, why they think the way they think. One reason why contrast is good to work with, is that we are affected by people who are different from ourselves. So, if you have an ongoing series where characters are going to go through a lot of changes, both the characters and the members of the audience can be moved to change their attitudes or values because of the effects of contrast and conflict that you have created.

The artist is the person trying to find that unique way of looking at something and the craftsperson is the one learning a lot of concepts. I don't call them rules or formulas, I call them concepts because there are many ways to apply them. Sometimes you take these concepts and they just don't apply to your story so you put them back in your tool chest. I think of concepts as this big tool chest, and when you run into a problem you take out each tool one by one and see if you can use it.

So, the concepts here are conflict and contrast. Conflict between characters in terms of thinking, acting, feeling, attitude, philosophy, values, decisions, actions, emotions and emotional responses. First make sure there is plenty of conflict in your story, then begin to think of your characters in terms of the contrast between them. Although nobody can guarantee success on any series, what I do believe I can guarantee with these concepts, is that you will never run out of material. If you really build conflict and contrast into your stories and into your pilot, in ten, twenty, thirty years, your story can still be going on.

SCRIPT AND PRODUCTION: THEIR INTERACTION

CORINNE HOLLINGWORTH

Since 1979, Corinne Hollingworth has worked in the BBC Drama Department, spending six years on "EastEnders" and subsequently joining the "Eldorado" production team as Series Producer. She is now executive producer of BBC TV's "Casualty".

When I was first approached about being a Specialist at the PILOTS workshop, I vacillated about accepting, thinking that perhaps my experience was too limited, having only ever produced two long-running serials or "soaps". But I reread the concept document, watched a considerable amount of television, and decided that drama is drama in whatever form. There may be a difference in degree between Alan Bleasdale's 10-part, one-hour weekly serial "**GBH**" and the thrice weekly "**Eldorado**"; but the same basics apply to both.

If there is one truth in producing television today, it is that there is never enough time or money to realise exactly what the writer intends and the director wishes. Programmes may be shorter or longer in length, have a greater or smaller budget, but the bottom line is always compromise. However, I don't believe that compromise should necessarily be viewed in a negative way. It can sometimes be a positive advantage rather than a limitation, in the way that the impressionist school of painting can be viewed as limiting choice and creativity, yet genius has resulted from its doctrine. So restrictions of time and money can create a situation whose very constraints can force a synthesis that may be magical.

I shall attempt to demonstrate this to you later by showing you some clips from "**Eldorado**", one of which successfully bears out the above and the other of which appears not to, as it is a compromise that did not work. But this was not because the concept was wrong, but because I made the wrong call! I simply got it wrong!

Another reason for my reticence about agreeing to be here was that I didn't know quite where to pitch my talk — you're obviously all professionals but your experiences are so disparate, not only due to different cultural backgrounds but also to the varying demands of your country's broadcasters. During my time living in Spain producing "**Eldorado**", for instance, I watched an evening of Spanish television and was staggered by how different it was from what we have on our screens in Britain.

> " *Good drama, well made, that deals with the basic human truths, must of necessity have a universal appeal.* "

But PILOTS has at its heart the idea of increasing the capacity of European series to "cross borders". And good drama, well made, that deals with the basic human truths, must of necessity have a universal appeal. Specific situations may vary from country to country, but life, death, birth, marriage, the struggle to survive and form meaningful relationships with other people, and above all laughter, are international.

Which brings me on to my other basic truth, which is that without the script there is nothing. Obviously the whole process starts with an idea, but many a good idea has foundered along the way because it has been badly realised. To go back one stage further, a good idea can be presented in a haphazard and confusing way so it is difficult to centre it properly and make the final product you want to make. However, there will inevitably be many discussions about your project with potential broadcasters, and you may be desperate to comply with what they suggest in order to get the commission.

But I think it is vital to remain true to your original idea. That's the programme you wanted to make, and although you have to compromise along the way, you also have to retain the integrity of that idea, otherwise you'll end up with a programme that you're not happy with, and the audience won't be happy either, because they'll sense a hole where the commitment and heart of it should be. The worst mistake, therefore, is to accept whatever limitations are placed on you simply to get the contract.

This, I believe, was one of the basic flaws of "**Eldorado**". The commission was finally given in January 1993 for a start in April of a series that was to run three times a week, so that's 156 half-hours of television. The size of the contract may have outweighed other considerations and the deal was made, despite the fact that there was insufficient time to build the set, let alone sort out all potential problem areas. As a result, chaos ensued and the programme suffered appallingly. This is not to say that you can't make adjustments as you go along — but do always remember why you wanted to do the project in the first place.

> " *Without the script there is nothing.* "

I'll give an example. I left "**EastEnders**" and the BBC because I had been approached by an independent production company who had been asked by Channel 4 to come up with a Bible for a twice-weekly soap to replace "**Brookside**", which at that time was not doing very well in the ratings. I duly did what I was asked, we submitted it to Channel 4, they liked the idea but by that stage (or so they told us) they had decided that maybe they didn't need a new soap after all, so could we develop a mini-series (along the same lines) instead.

We did this and, of course, they turned it down because the idea had been right and appropriate for a long-running serial, where characters develop slowly and the plot unfolds around the character, but not necessarily right for a mini-series. There the story is initially the most important thing, and generally it's through that hook that you get your audience interested in the characters. In a tri-weekly it's the other way round — you have to establish the characters, and you do that by making them familiar and accessible, identifiable, vulnerable and sympathetic. So character development in a mini-series has to be incredibly fast, because instead of 104 or 156 episodes, you have three or four.

I'll never do that again. I knew it was the wrong thing to do and that we were losing any centre the programme had by trying to constrain it, but we went through hoops trying to find a synthesis that was acceptable to all of us, and it never worked. It's worthwhile being cautious about mutating one thing into another.

Although my brief is to deal with the translation of the script into a finished programme, I would like to stress here that the script is the most important thing. If you get that right, you are half-way there. In many ways, it is much more difficult to write an episode of a series or long-running serial than it is to have an original one-off idea where you have, initially at least, complete autonomy to do what you wish. If you are asked to write an episode of any long-runner you have tremendous restrictions placed on you in terms of having to pick up storylines (that maybe you find it difficult to engage with), write to a precise document outlining where the epiosde must start and finish, and sometimes what happens along the way as well, pick up the exact continuity of characters which necessitates a pretty thorough knowledge of preceding episodes and write to a specific format with (generally) limitations of cast numbers, the amount of location work, the sets available and restrictions of transmission slot.

> " It is much more difficult to write an episode of a series or long-running serial than it is to have an original one-off idea. "

It is, ultimately, a corporate effort between the writer, script editor and producer. And it depends on a strong relationship having been formed between the three, built on mutual respect and trust, because the writer has to entrust his or her baby to a script editor, and the producer has to entrust his or her belief to the script editor, and then the director comes in as well. So it depends on all parties deciding what the essence of the script is to be. And there is no point continuing to work with people if you don't trust them.

I have been in the situation where I've had a script editor who was an extremely nice person but not the right one for the job. I kept asking her to address certain things in the scripts, and it was done but not in the way I envisaged it, so after a few weeks I realised that we were never going to collaborate successfully. It makes the job almost impossible in such circumstances and, as everybody has different practices, you have to arrive at a consensus of how you want to work on a project, and as the producer you have to lead that whole process because ultimately you carry the can.

In my experience there are three questions that need to be applied to any script that is about to be produced as part of a long-running serial, and they are:

1. Is the story told in the best possible way?

2. Can it be achieved within the available budget?

3. Is all the content absolutely necessary to the story and appropriate for its transmission slot?

I don't really want to deal with point 1 in detail because I'm sure that was covered by Lilie Ferrari in her session (see "Tightrope-walking: The Script Editor"). However I have included it because it is important

> " *The writer has to entrust his or her baby to a script editor, and the producer has to entrust his or her belief to the script editor* "

that you realise that although my main preoccupation is to deal with the practicalities of translating a script into a programme that is on budget, as a producer I am ultimately responsible for the overall programme, I'm totally committed to the project and want it to be as good and as true as it possibly can.

Yet it is also my responsibility to work within certain parameters. Whenever I have worked on series, I have treated each individual episode as though it is a "Play for Today", or a one-off "Screen One" (a BBC1 TV movie), simply because, although it's part of a continuum, you have to look at that episode, ask if it has a beginning, a middle and an end, are there arcs in the story, do the characters progress, is there a progression in the story from the beginning to the end? The episode has to stand by itself as something that can be treated as a complete entity, and that means a lot of work. You have to take into account episodes that have already been written which will come afterwards, and endless episodes before that have to be referred to.

But I think it vital not to diminish the input of any one episode as just being part of a serial. For my money, every episode of **"EastEnders"**, **"Eldorado"** and **"Coronation Street"** is as important as any one-off, and you owe it to the audience to give the best you possibly can.

So I'll go straight on to point two — "Can the episode be achieved within the available budget?" And for this I need to look at three major areas: complexity of scenes, including numbers of cast; extent of location material; and extent of night shooting. The one thing I learned very early on when I was an Associate Producer controlling the budget on **"EastEnders"**, is that with night shooting you think of the number of hours it will take, and then double, or treble it. It is an incredibly slow process technically, because of the problems of 'seeing' the action. How do you make it look realistic and yet not annoy the audience with too little light, so they have to strain to see what is on screen? Psychologically it is difficult because your crew and actors are working unsocial hours and, unless you're shooting in a very hot climate, it's generally bloody cold.

If you *are* shooting at night in a country where night falls late, your available shooting time will be reduced radically anyway, so you're between a rock and a hard place. Even on a soap, where the shooting ratio is generally very high, depending on the complexity of the scene, it can take three hours to shoot two minutes of screen time, but during the daytime on **"Eldorado"** we averaged between 12 and 18 minutes a day, using two cameras, and I don't believe that the quality suffered from speed in this particular case.

I'd like to show you an example of some night shooting on **"Eldorado"**. The director had four hours to shoot; she planned to do 25 set-ups and had to compromise on about eight. You have a copy of the sequence in front of you (see pages 148 to 150) and, as you'll see, her problems were compounded by the fact that it was an "action" sequence with lots of cars, which are notorious for breaking down as soon as they are used. If you look at the written scenes, you'll see that they contained a lot more detail than actually showed in the final product. This was a first-time director doing the shoot and I think she did an incredible job. After three hours and only two set-ups we had to make some very quick decisions about what could go, and in fact some shots were done at another time. We did lose some of the sequence simply because there wasn't the time, but I believe we had already achieved the essence of the scene. In an ideal world it would have been great to have had more time, but I don't know that the scenes would inevitably have been that much better.

On the same theme as that, I'll show you a scene from Episode 154 of "**Eldorado**" (see pages 150 to 152). You have the original scene in front of you plus the compromised scene. Just to give a bit of background detail: the original ending to this episode was to have been Trish and Alex with Trish telling Alex she had to go back to Spain, but I felt this was rather weak. The script editor and I discussed it and we felt we needed to add a bit of dramatic action to the episode, and the conclusion we arrived at was that we should develop the Drew/Marcus story as we had already storylined Drew in the next episode arriving home with an injury of some sort (this to act as a catalyst for the main story leading to the end of the series). So we decided to see the incident where Drew is injured — initially it was to be a daytime scene but then we had to justify Drew being away from home all night, partially to help another story that needed a passage of time, so a decision was made to set it at night.

When the script arrived, I thought the sequence could work very well but realised it would be expensive, so I had it costed by our production supervisor who came back panic-stricken talking of six boats, exorbitant costs plus the fact that it would take at least six hours to shoot in an already overcrowded schedule. So I said no, we'd think again. And what you're about to see is the result of that decision.

Now without recriminating too much about it, I take full responsibility for the failure of this sequence. I made a mistake. The director didn't help but the sequence looks like it was made on a shoestring, and is, above all, a cheat. And this is where we come to our third point — is the content necessary to the story and is it appropriate for its transmission slot? In this instance, yes, it was necessary, and I should have fought for it from an editorial standpoint. But I didn't. My mistake and the audience's loss. I'll show you a sequence now where I did fight and we arrived at a good and reasonably-priced solution.

There is a sequence of scenes from the last episode involving Marcus' car being blown up. Obviously this had always been in the storyline, but there are ways of telling this story without necessarily seeing the actual car blow up. I felt that in order to make the audience believe the story we were telling, we needed the shock of the explosion. But there were problems. The car had been lent to us by Renault and its list price was £35,000 — a sum that I didn't really feel we were justified in blowing up. Plus you only get one go at this sort of sequence.

The solution to the dilemma was to find a shell of a car of the same dimensions, spray it and modify it, which I think the art department did superbly. In the edit we then did a fast mix from the real car to the fake, the explosion happening on the mix and what you saw was the result. The shell cost approximately £200. We had to pay for the special effects but the whole thing cannot have cost more than £3,000. So it can be done!

The last aspect of my third point is the appropriateness of the material for the transmission slot. In my experience, writers often want to push the boundaries further than is acceptable to the establishment. I'm sure you have equivalents in your own countries, but in Britain there is what is known as the 9 o'clock watershed, the notion being that before that time children will be watching and therefore certain things cannot be shown or said, as these children might be corrupted. After that, the world's your oyster, almost, but the restrictions on language and violence particularly are getting stricter and stricter.

When I first started on soaps, a certain amount of bad language and violence was acceptable. This has now changed, and quite recently I did an episode of "**Eldorado**" where Marcus grabs Pilar and she bites his wrist, which I thought was acceptable, as did the Executive Producer. But the Head of Series (in the light of much recent publicity and political debate about the level of violence on television) insisted it be cut. After a short fight I agreed. There are certain battles it is simply not worth waging. And I took out such a small amount that it made no difference to the scene anyway. The writer of a subsequent epiosde wrote a much more violent scene than the one I had already tampered with, and as I knew the consequences if we included it, we toned it down and made the violence implicit rather than explicit at the editing stage.

To conclude — yes, compromises have to be made all along the way, and the producer is the one who must call the shots: my philosophy is that in the majority of cases, bad language and explicit violence at 7 pm are unnecessary. If the scene is well played and directed it will be pregnant with tension anyway and on the odd occasion when it is necessary, I will be in a strong position to fight for it because I haven't been profligate beforehand.

There is almost always an acceptable solution to any problem, if you are prepared to look for it. The answer is to be flexible and to have an understanding of the production process and, above all, to work with people you admire and trust because television is about communication, and that doesn't mean just communicating with the audience. It means at every stage, the writer, script editor, producer and the director getting together and talking to ensure that the initial concept remains intact. It's about belief and commitment to an idea — and when you get it right it's the best industry in the world in which to work. When you get it wrong, well... let's hope none of you will.

> **" Compromises have to be made all along the way. "**

EXAMPLE 1

Scene 2 Ext.

SET ROAD (LOCATION) NIGHT

(23.01)

(Cut to close shot of Marcus: staring out through the windscreen of his car.

Then cut to a group of Spaniards standing in front of him on road, blocking his path and carrying an assortment of knifes, large mallets. Ahead of them are parked cars, also blocking the road.)

Scene 4 Ext.

SET ROAD (LOCATION) NIGHT

(23.02)

(Inside his car, Marcus: flicks a switch activating the central locking, a loud clunk sounding as the bolts lock into place on the two doors.

Then Marcus slams the car into reverse, twisting back in his seat and gunning the accelerator, powering the car away from the watching Spaniards; but before Marcus has reversed more than a few feet he slams his brakes on as headlights suddenly appear behind him.

Another set of headlights appear behind the first pair, then another, making three cars in all. The cars stop as they reach Marcus, blocking his exit from the rear.

Marcus looks at the grouped headlights behind him, then turns back in his seat to face the Spaniards once again.

Pilar's husband, Sergio, now emerges from the middle of the waiting, watching group and stands, facing Marcus.)

Scene 8 Ext.

SET ROAD (LOCATION) NIGHT

(23.03)

(Back on the deserted road, blazing headlights lighting the scene, the Spaniards are now circling Marcus' car, walking slowly around and around it; Sergio stands in front of the car, staring in at Marcus.)

Scene 12 Ext.

SET ROAD (LOCATION) NIGHT

(23.04)

(The Spaniards are still circling around and around Marcus' car, hunters stalking their prey. Hold scene for moment.

Perhaps Marcus now reaches for his phone to summon help but then there's a loud explosion of glass close at hand as Sergio smashes the side window on the driver's side.

Sergio looks in at Marcus, nothing now between them. Hold moment as Sergio stares at Marcus, Marcus stares back at him.

Sergio turns to his friends and nods. The friends now produce large knives, hold them up in full view of Marcus.

Hold on Marcus for moment.

Then the Spaniards plunge the knives into each of the car tyres in turn, great explosions of air now hissing into the night as each tyre collapses.

Sergio looks at Marcus again, gives him a last ironic mock-salute, then joins his friends who are all now moving back towards their cars, laughing, clapping each other on the back.

Cut back to and hold on a now-shaking Marcus watching them go.)

Scene 15 Ext.

SET ROAD (LOCATION) NIGHT

(23.08)

(Marcus: sits in car, immobile, the road ahead of him deserted now, Marcus staring out through the windscreen. Then he gets out and stares down at the slashed tyres. Grabs mobile phone — tries to dial — it doesn't work. Flat batteries? This is the last straw. Marcus throws it angrily back in the car and looks around desperately.)

Scene 20A Ext.

SET ROAD (LOCATION) NIGHT

(23.15)

(Marcus: walks grimly along the side of the road. Headlights appear in the distance. He looks round, excited. The car approaches. Marcus sticks out his thumb, but the car roars past. Marcus kicks the ground angrily and looks around him in desperation.)

EXAMPLE 2

Scene 27 Ext.

SET MARCUS' BOAT / OPEN SEA

(LOCATION) DAY (20.30)

(Drew and the other crew member stare through darkness. Drew uses binoculars.)

Drew: Here she comes. A light to port. There, look.

(We see, from their pov, an approaching light. The light of a boat. Nothing more than a glimmer but advancing steadily.

Marcus is speaking to it over radio.)

Marcus: (Into radio) I want all the men on deck, and the dinghy ready in the water now. I want this whole operation over in five minutes Roger.

(Crackle.)

Radio voice from other end: Approaching 10 degrees starboard (please insert correct nautical term here) slowing to three knots.

Marcus: (To Drew and Crew) Get ready.

(See Crew get rope ladder out, see Drew remove a section of deck rail.

See other boat drawing near enough to see. And behind the lights, standing on deck, a dozen or so anxious looking Moroccans holding bundles. Illegal immigrants.)

Scene 29 Ext.

SET MARCUS' BOAT (LOCATION)

DAY (20.35)

(The two boats are now close to each other and the dinghy has made one journey between them bringing the skipper and three of the Moroccans to Marcus' boat.

The dinghy is just setting off again when they hear the engine of a third boat, approaching at speed and with no lights...

Pandemonium... The three Moroccans are bundled back into the dinghy and cast off to row back on their own to the other boat. (Where the other Moroccans are waiting.)

As Marcus starts their engine for a quick getaway, Drew is trying, with difficulty, to replace the deckrail. But the police launch is too quick for them

There are shouted instructions to "stop and be boarded" coming from the launch.

Drew looks frantically across at the police launch and at Marcus, who is steering the boat away. Drew clearly thinks they should stop and starts to move towards Marcus to get him to do this.

Marcus takes no notice. The police open fire.

Drew is hit, staggers back...)

END OF EPISODE 154

COMPROMISE SCENE 29

Scene 29 Ext.

SET MARCUS' BOAT (LOCATION)

NIGHT (22.00)

(On Marcus steering the boat at speed through the water. He looks around him and calls a member of Crew to steer for him. He moves along the gangway towards the cabin and lets himself in. He looks across at Drew who is slumped in a chair, holding his arm, through the fingers of his hand blood is oozing. The look which is exchanged between him and Marcus is one of cold hatred. Marcus doesn't approach Drew but returns on deck. We stay with Drew nursing his gunshot wound.)

END OF EPISODE 154

LIFE'S A PITCH!

JULIAN FRIEDMANN

Joint managing director of Blake Friedmann Literary Agency, Head of Studies and Initiator of PILOTS, a UK advisor to the European Film College, and author of a forthcoming book on the business of scriptwriting.

Before you have to make a verbal pitch, you can and should pre-pare written pitches, but what I want to talk about here is 'verbal' pitching. This is the time when writers or producers have to get up on the stage and perform.

We do not work in a 'pitching culture' in Europe. But pitching is an essential part of the professionalism of writers, of script edi-tors, and of producers, and good projects are too often rejected because the 'buyer' loses confidence in the pitcher.

But the good news is that there are specific preparations you can make to improve your verbal pitching. Writers and producers rarely put as much effort into preparing *themselves* as they do into preparing their projects. But you are part of the pitch, and you can easily let yourself down.

Once you understand why so many people pitch badly at really important meetings, you can do something to prevent yourself from doing it. You must have all had the experience: to come out of a meeting *knowing* you performed badly.

You can significantly improve your pitch simply by a better understanding of the significance of non-verbal communication. You can find out how you can *tell* when to stop talking, or when to change direction. You can learn how to *sell* the story, rather than just *tell* the story. And you can learn how to control the direction of a meeting, so that you can get much more out of it.

Writers are constantly pressurised to write good scripts... but where does the preparation for delivering a good pitch come from? And how often are writers let down because their producer makes a bad pitch despite the fact that it is a wonderful script?

* * * * *

In the Altman film "**The Player**", people really do pitch like that, and we will look at some examples of typical Hollywood pitch lines later. But in Europe there simply isn't a pitching culture. This applies both to those pitching *and* to those listening to the pitches.

> *" Good projects are too often rejected because the 'buyer' loses confidence in the pitcher. "*

What this means is that producers and broadcasters in Europe are probably less interested in the pitch itself, and probably more interested in who you are and what you've done in the past, than their counterparts in America. Having never done anything in Los Angeles is the equivalent to never having failed.

But if you are aware, as you should be, that a good idea will often be rejected because the buyer does not like or respect or have confidence in the pitcher, you will realise how important performing on the day is.

It's also worth remembering that in our industry what is said is often not believed to be true. For example, the sentence, "I have a deal" usually means "I have had a conversation". So there's a lot of scepticism that you have to overcome with your verbal pitch.

When you pitch, you don't pitch films or programmes, you pitch ideas or packages. Similarly, your first draft script is just a *proposal*, not a shooting script.

You should be able to pitch something in under a minute. A minute is a long time to listen. So prior to making a pitch you should be able to distil the essentials of your project down to the minimum necessary to tell the listener the following:

1. What it is about (you do not need to tell the story, just what sort of story or programme it is).

2. Why it will appeal to audiences and to which audiences it will appeal.

3. And, particularly if you are the producer, where you hope the finance will come from.

Some of the activity writers and producers are inevitably involved in *is* packaging. It is what writers and producers and film-makers do, without necessarily calling it that.

To do this successfully you must know your way around the players and around the industry. You cannot do this if you are an amateur, which is what many good writers are, if they confine their professional activities purely to writing.

> " *There's a lot of scepticism that you have to overcome with your verbal pitch.* "

The term 'packaging' reached its ultimate expression in the methods used by the biggest Hollywood agencies in bringing together their own clients (producer, writer, director and stars) in a package which they take to the studio to wholly finance.

The package is *so* bankable that the studio cannot refuse, whatever the budget. Or it may be that the studio is so anxious for one element in the package that they are effectively forced to take all the rest. This is the ultimate deal-led approach to financing; it has some advantages and many disadvantages.

I would like us to consider these activities under three headings: the SCRIPT, the PACKAGE and the PITCH, before we run through five checklists that should provide you with much of what you need to know to improve your pitching.

THE SCRIPT

The 'package' usually starts with an idea or a script. I believe that it is best for us to concentrate on the script as the starting point, with the other elements following. So let me make a few provocative comments about the problems that sometimes occur in the relationship between producers and writers.

- Producers often think that because they are paying, they know best about the writer and the script.

- Producers in Europe usually do not invest enough money or time in the development and rewriting of the scripts they want to produce.

- Producers often select the wrong writer: eg. commission an adaptation from a writer good at original scripts or an original script from a writer good at adaptations.

- Producers are seldom trained to do script analyses and are often not good at talking to writers.

> " *Producers in Europe usually do not invest enough money or time in the development and rewriting of the scripts they want to produce.* "

- Producers too often, if they can afford it, rely on big-name writers who are inappropriate (perhaps on the basis that if a script is lousy the producer cannot be blamed since the writer was so experienced...).

- Producers are often more interested in the deal than the script: too many producers behave as if the definition of a producer is someone who produces money.

Fortunately there are some very good producers. But the point is that writers have little *real* control over the production of their scripts and are seldom encouraged by producers to get involved in any way other than just as a writer-for-hire.

Writers can be as problematic as producers. For a start they too often think that because they thought of an idea, it's *worth writing*; they too rarely research the market adequately; they seldom try to understand enough about the problems faced by the producer in raising the money for the film or series written by the writer.

Because of this, producers and writers often fail to benefit from the real contribution the other might have been able to make. Remember, if you are a producer who is commissioning a writer (or indeed if you are a writer remember these points too):

- Be sure you know what you want from the writer. The writer must be sure s/he knows what *is* wanted.

- Be sure you are clear in briefing the writer (always follow up with written confirmation; ask the writer to do the same — you will be amazed at how often the writer has not understood what you think is clear or vice versa, and it may be your fault).

- If the writer fails to deliver an acceptable rewrite after you have clearly explained what is wrong with the current draft, cut your losses and get another writer. Be sure your contract with the writer takes this possibility into account. If the idea is an original idea from the writer, this may be difficult — as it should be.

> " *Why are so many bad scripts filmed?* "

A good script, a good story, is the most important element in the package. A great director, a great actor or actress, cannot rescue a bad script. Unfortunately in reality a too-common definition of a good script is: one that raises money. However, money does not guarantee a good film. And getting the script right is always one of the least expensive items in the budget.

So why are so many bad scripts filmed? I believe it is because too many producers have not learned to read scripts, and the tremendous and admirable effort they put into raising the finance and putting the deals together results in a danger of their paying too little attention to the script once the money has been found. Writers, directors and agents who do the same are also to blame.

THE PACKAGE

The essence of packaging is the delicate balance between form, content and cost. One definition of packaging is: to raise the finance by identifying what elements are needed in what order. In other words, by bringing the elements you require together in a particular order you can get more or less control and power over your project.

This is producer's work, but I think we should look at this, because writers need much greater knowledge of what producers do.

Anybody can package. A producer can be a packager or vice-versa. Writers can and should learn to package. Your package may be just a fantasy, a wish-list, but it shows you were thinking through the implications of your script for the series or film.

All it involves is persuasion, selling, and perhaps negotiation. Remember, the purpose is simply to get money from someone. The key questions are: what do you think you're giving them for the money and what do they think they're getting for it?

You need, therefore, to know:

- What elements are needed in what order to raise the finance? Unless you know how to negotiate, get someone better at it than you are to do it for you, or learn.

- You need to know how to get into a position of strength, to keep creative control (or, again, get someone better at it than you to represent you).

- You need to know things like the fact that coproduction generally requires higher pre- *and* post-production costs.

- You need to know how to use casting and locations to raise money.

- You need to know how to obtain bankable assets. If a producer can't afford the best possible writer s/he should try harder to find a way of getting the best writer by negotiating a different sort of deal (for example, a smaller advance with increased backend pay-ment — it's easier to pay more when it's not your money, and by the time you raise the final part of your budget it certainly should not be your money).

- You need to know why it is such a high risk if you are writer, pro-ducer and director. The answer is that all decisions devolve onto you and few investors will believe you are capable of being suffi-ciently objective to take care of their investment. Therefore you should be very aware of how difficult it is to be critical of yourself and how important it is to impose genuine self-censorship ('Kill the darlings'). In other words, in packaging always try to add assets to your package and eliminate liabilities (which more often than not are other people's egos, and sometimes your own).

- You need to know why not to rely on friends/jobs for the boys. The art of delegation is to delegate to people better than you.

- You need to know that you can usually only sell marquee names to American networks and studios, and if you need the sort of budget that only they tend to invest in and you are not really well known and do not have a track record, perhaps you should re-think your ambitions.

- You need to know how to be flexible: Berndt Eichinger gave a good example of packaging from "The Name of the Rose": he changed the minimum guarantee distribution arrangement on two territories so that the film, from a French and Italian point of view, was a coproduction which made it easier to sell to French and Italian audiences.

- You need to know that good actors look at scripts not to count their lines but to see what there is for them to do when they are not speaking (ie. when they are acting). Hitchcock once said, 'The best screen actor is that person who can do nothing extremely well".

You may think that all this has little to do with writing scripts, but it has a lot to do with pitching, which in turn is relevant to your ability to sell yourself.

THE PITCH

Once you've assembled your package, you can start to 'sell' it and yourself. This will inevitably involve verbal pitching.

An analysis of classical 'oratory' comes up with a number of basic principles:

- Decide what you think (most people don't really know — they only think they do).

- Select your arguments.

- Anticipate your opponent's arguments (think Devil's Advocate).

- Put your arguments in order (work out a manipulative game-plan).

- Work out your method of presentation:

  - do you memorise — can you?
  - do you have notes — should you?
  - what does your voice sound like — could it be improved?
  - and so on.

PITCH EXAMPLES

These are well-known feature films — but the principle is the same for TV drama (which doesn't promote itself so actively). A full pitch is different from a story concept 'pitch line'. A pitch line could be: 'This is a story about _____ who _____.". You should be able to reduce every proposal to that. It's difficult to be so succinct, which is why I want to concentrate on it for a moment.

I am going to read out a few pitch lines from well-known movies. A useful exercise is to guess the title of the film. Or test yourself and friends with the film and guess the pitch line.

"A husband, a wife, a billionaire, a proposal" ("**Indecent Proposal**", Adrian Lyne, Robert Redford, Demi Moore).

"The adventures of an ordinary man at war with the everyday world" ("**Falling Down**", Michael Douglas).

"He left behind everything he knew for the only thing he ever wanted" ("**Far and Away**", Tom Cruise, Nicole Kidman, director Ron Howard).

"In space, no one can hear you scream!" ("**Alien**")

"This is Benjamin... He's a little worried about his future!" ("**The Graduate**").

"They're young... They're in love... And they kill people!" ("**Bonnie and Clyde**").

"Just when you thought it was safe to go back in the water" ("**Jaws 2**").

"There are three sides to this love story" ("**Kramer vs. Kramer**").

"Love means never having to say you're sorry" ("**Love Story**").

"He would do anything to help her live. But would he help her die?" ("**When the Time Comes**", starring Bonnie Bedelia, produced by Sherry Lansing, about euthanasia).

"We are not alone" ("**Close Encounters of the Third Kind**").

"You don't assign him to murder cases — you just turn him loose" ("**Dirty Harry**")

"A man can't get a job so he dresses up as a woman then falls in love with someone who doesn't know he's really a man." (Not "**Some Like it Hot**" but "**Tootsie**").

"White pizza in black Brooklyn" ("**Do the Right Thing**").

> " **The person you're pitching to wants to know that you are passionate about this particular project.** "

Hollywood is the spiritual home of the pitch. There are a lot of bizarre stories that have come out of Hollywood, and there are all sorts of rules that people are forever telling you about pitching. Although some of them are enlightening, I think it is better if you are able to think on your feet, and respond to each pitching situation rather than depend on hard and fast rules.

One of the most important things to remember about a pitch — it's not really a 'rule' — is passion. The person you're pitching to wants to know that you are passionate about this particular project. Which is why if you go in with five or ten ideas it begins to look as though you are promiscuous or fickle, and you're not interested in a serious relationship.

Pitching really evolved when television changed Hollywood. When they had the writers' buildings where writers were paid salaries to sit and write, it wasn't the writers who went in and pitched — it was the producers who told the writers what to write. Once television emerged, with a huge increase in the number of programmes needed, the producers didn't have the time to come up with the storylines or even read the detailed long-form treatments which writers produced. So writers began to be asked to sum up briefly what it was they were going to do.

You've got to remember that a major studio in Hollywood could receive anything between 40-50,000 pitches or proposals a year. Yet they probably don't make more than 10 or 12 movies a year. That is, in a nutshell, why writers are at the bottom of the totem pole and often get a really raw deal. The ratio in Europe for long-running series is also rather depressing.

It is often said that you should be able to pitch in 60 seconds. Some people say you should be able to do it in 15 seconds. Short is always better than long. After all, if they like what they have heard but want more detail, they'll ask. A short pitch, particularly a good one, is likely to be more memorable than a long one, even if it, too, is good.

> *" You should be able to pitch in 60 seconds. Some people say you should be able to do it in 15 seconds. "*

But be prepared: if the listeners look bored don't just continue, lift your voice, your passion, or even point out that it doesn't seem suitable for them. So have a back-up ready. Avoid too many details: this is called 'sketching the big picture'. In other words, use broad brushstrokes rather than fine detailed lines.

Remember that a pitch is not a story. It's a concept and can't therefore go into detail about characters. That's what a script does. Some people say character-driven movies like "**Terms of Endearment**" or "**Ordinary People**" are more difficult to pitch, which is why you can sometimes get round that by drawing a parallel between your story and another film or series that everyone knows.

Another desirable strategy is to try to pitch to somebody who can say yes. Unfortunately that's not always possible and you have to pitch to somebody who has access to somebody who can say yes.

However, the bottom line is that a good pitch may get you a deal but it won't get your film or programme made. If you are very adept at coming up with high concept ideas, good at articulating them and persuading people that they're worth doing, but you're not a good enough writer, then perhaps you should be a producer.

There is not much point pitching yourself as a writer if you can't write. You *must* have material *ready* to follow up your pitch meeting. A good pitch won't help you write a better script, unless you already write well.

Be *enthusiastic*. Show your passion for the story. You've only got a couple of minutes!

Remember — whatever anyone else tells you — that the story is not as important as the way you tell it. So, here are the checklists which should help you *tell* the story — however good or bad it is — as well as possible.

> " *Try to pitch to somebody who can say yes.* "

THE CHECKLISTS

The five checklists are:

1. Know yourself
2. Know them
3. Non-verbal communication
4. The pitch
5. Handling meetings

These checklists will cover most of the points you should be aware of before you go into a pitch meeting.

Checklist 1: Know Yourself

1. What is your perception of how you pitch? Think about it. Find out about it — use a mirror, friends or a video camera.

2. Much more effort goes into the preparation of projects than one-self, so prepare yourself. What reaction do you normally bring out in others? What is your perception of your strengths and weaknesses? As a negotiator/as a team member?

3. Learn negotiating techniques — the art of pitching almost always involves negotiating. It involves your reacting to their reactions, and those techniques are well-articulated in dozens of books.

4. Learn to relax — breathing exercises, a good night's sleep before you go in, and a healthy dose of fatalism, will all help your performance on the day.

When people are very nervous, oxygen is redirected to the muscles so they see and hear better but don't necessarily speak more clearly. The brain decides, in a fight or flight situation, that you don't need continuous logical thought. In order to counteract this, make sure you breathe deeply and properly to get more oxygen to the brain. How often have you come out of a meeting knowing you've pitched or dealt with the questions really badly, although you had all the information to deal with it well? The probable cause is lack of oxygen in the brain.

Checklist 2: Know Them

1. Know who they are: names, positions, track records. Offer a business card to each person you are pitching to, so you get theirs.

2. Know what they've done: how well it performed, even what their specific role in it was.

3. Know what they are looking for.

4. Know what they can pay and have paid in the past.

Checklist 3: Non-Verbal Communication

1. Shaking hands is very important: but not too hard, although do it decisively. Don't seem limp or timid.

2. You give out and perceive signals from a very early age. Body language is something you ought to know about if you want to win. There are no books about body language in film and television pitch meetings, but there are many about body language in general, so read at least one.

3. Try and make direct eye contact and open gestures: eg. with your hands open rather than folding your arms tightly across your chest.

4. Leaning towards someone, not away from them, is more likely to make them feel you are engaging with them.

5. Mirroring their behaviour and body language can also be subliminally flattering. It's not usually done consciously, and it's interesting to observe it.

6. Making notes about what they're saying will give them a sense of being important and being taken seriously.

Checklist 4: The Pitch

1. Passion and clarity are the two most important qualities in your 60 seconds.

2. Know in advance how much you should say.

3. Learn to be very aware of whether you are running over. Know when to stop (you do this by watching and listening to them).

4. Don't over-sell (believing that they really need your series, your episode or your film is arrogant).

> " *The pitch should sell the story whereas the treatment should tell the story.* "

5. High concept means something easily grasped. Can you find a way of putting your project into those terms?

6. The pitch should sell the story whereas the treatment should tell the story. Don't confuse the two. Never get into the boring 'and then... and then... and then' storytelling rut. It's deadly to listen to.

7. Remember the three rules of storytelling and therefore pitching (perhaps these *are* rules):

   a) what it is about?
   b) why and to whom will it appeal?
   c) where will the finance come from?

Checklist 5: Handling Meetings

1. Establish rapport at the very beginning of the meeting by asking them questions about themselves, their company, their films or programmes, their country. It's perfectly OK to spend at least the first five minutes doing this — in other words, get them to pitch themselves to you. It breaks the ice, it gives you great leads and cues.

2. Do you know how to control the direction of a meeting? There are *no* rules, but it's about intelligence, perception, and the ability to think fast on your feet. If you are bad at it, get someone else to do it with or for you.

3. Do you know how to be a good listener?

4. Do you know how to be a perceptive watcher? Can you observe while are you talking *and* listening? In other words, can you stand back a bit while in full flow?

5. If they don't speak your language well make sure you speak slowly and clearly.

6. If they ask difficult questions keep your integrity by saying you'll get back to them later on with the answer, rather than just lying and possibly being caught out.

> **" The story is not as important as the way you tell it. "**

7. Don't react negatively to criticism: say 'that's interesting and I'll certainly think about it', even if you think it's not interesting or just plain stupid. Be cool.

8. Encourage criticism and frankness. Start by emphasising that you *really* want them to tell you what they think.

9. Finally, remember that you are not a one-story writer or producer.

A lousy story and a bad pitch can sometimes still get you a result if they think you are someone they can work with. I think it was William Goldman who once described Hollywood as being 'about your *next* project'. So don't put all the emphasis on this one. Always try to open doors for yourself. You are part of the pitch. But it's what most writers and most producers forget as they invest their time in working on the story.

The story is not as important as the way you tell it. A mediocre story in the hands of a great writer will be more successful than a great story in the hands of a mediocre writer. Being able to pitch well will almost certainly have a beneficial effect on your ability to write a good script. If you have the talent.

BROADCASTING TRENDS

ROBERTO PACE

Roberto Pace has been a scriptwriter, story editor, director, actor and independent producer for many film and TV productions.
He is responsible for fiction at RAI 1 and head of the Programme Committee and Development Fund of the ECA.

Once upon a time, perhaps 20-25 years ago, only public service television existed in Europe. The mandate, the remit, of public service television was to serve a homogeneous, or what was assumed to be a homogeneous, national audience. The definition of the audience was simply the family in its three generations: the parents, the children and the elderly.

The family was the basis of the conception of the audience. The united family was the target for public service television. And this family audience was offered programmes which were designed around qualities the BBC had taught the rest of Europe: they were entertaining, instructive and informative.

At this time, then, you believed you had a very clear idea of what the audience was and how to serve it. All the programmes, from drama to news to light entertainment, were produced strictly in-house by the channel, in the studio owned by the channel, and this meant there was an absolute overlap of identity between the producer and the distributor. There was no difference. And of course the problems of international co-production were virtually non-existent, since 99% of the programmes were financed by the channel itself with the financing gathered within the country, and no need to obtain any money from outside.

Bartering between channels was very rare, because it was not necessary. There was a small amount of co-operation between public service television organizations, an association had been set up called the EBU, which still exists, and they had some exchange in terms of news programmes and sports programmes, but almost nothing in drama.

What happened then? With the advent of commercial television and competition, the situation changed dramatically. First of all you have to assume that the money to be spent in television is just one pot, enlargeable to a certain extent, but after that it's finished. So the same pot was to be divided amongst several players, which meant less money for the public service channels because more players were playing the same game. What did that mean? That meant the position of the channel changed radically, and the so-called theory of the North-West Passage was born.

The North-West Passage Theory, which grew out of market television, is based on a graphic representation of television viewers which plots sex and age against educational level. The theory shows that channels want to end up in the top left-hand corner of the diagram, the segment which is occupied mainly by less-educated women which they believe offers the greatest potential for growth. It is where household products and a wide range of consumer goods can be advertised. And it is the segment where, in the last five years, all the general broadcasters, certainly in France, Germany and Italy, have tried to locate themselves, at the expense of the other three sectors of the market.

For another difference between the past and the present, you could look at types of programmes. In the beginning we had only national programmes produced in-house but now we have an international variety. Why? Because in-house production entered a serious crisis when the commercial channels in the market acquired a large amount of American and foreign programmes, better produced and devised, and much more effective in terms of audience results than the in-house programmes. If in 1971 a one-hour, in-house production in Germany cost 500,000 DM, you could buy a better — to some a more beautiful programme — for 50,000 DM. Of course this was the only way for commercial private broadcasters to enter the market: they didn't have in-house facilities and it was their only way of competing.

A second consideration was general lack of money, the pot being enlargeable but finite. Both commercial broadcasters and public service broadcasters needed to find more money to have the same amount of hours to transmit. If you have to provide at least 50 nights of prime-time drama, and you have only half the money necessary, this is a big incentive to go for co-production.

At the very beginning co-production was something rather easy to do. Let me try and explain what it was like. We have a programme, let's say in Italy, for which we have 75% of the budget. Then they have a programme in Britain for which they have 75% of the budget. The two commissioning editors know each other because of normal commercial relationships and one says "Look, I have a beautiful programme. I just need 25% to produce it." And the other says "Yes, but I have another beautiful programme and I need another 25% to produce it." So one invests 25% in the other and vice versa. It's just an exchange of budgets, it doesn't really increase the production budget of either of the programmes. This was the so-called twinning strategy, twinning because they tried to make twins out of different, sometimes very different, programmes.

This was the most archaic form of doing co-production. Recently different kinds of co-production have been developed such as co-financing. There is the famous BBC approach, especially with regard to the Continent: "You give us the money, we'll make the programme." This meant the least possible creative input from the Continental broadcasters. It was a form which worked very well in documentary films, for instance, where everybody recognized the expertise of the BBC staff, and so they were happy to co-finance the programme in that way.

Another method of co-production was to create a sort of permanent framework, with a given budget and the possibility of producing a given number of hours per year. The European Co-production Association falls into this category and the combination of Fininvest, Betataurus and TF1 is trying to do the same thing.

This is a very brief history of co-production. What has it meant for the present, before we even speak about the future? The first thing that has been affected is the programme schedule. The programme schedule today is very different to what it was in the past. There is a large amount of flexibility. Very stabilised, very rigid programme formats are no longer viable in the present market. Long-running series are very difficult to place, at least in the Continental programme schedule. The one-hour format has virtually disappeared from France, Italy, Spain and even Germany, where ZDF has changed its one-hour programme slot in prime-time to 90 minutes.

Why? Because the commercial channels in all the countries affected by severe deregulation and by competition between public service television and commercial television used to be able, because of financing and maybe because they were more intelligent, to acquire a large number of feature films in order to compete effectively against their public service rivals. This means that in Italy, for instance, you have some 20-25 feature films being shown per night.

> **" The television movie as a format is one of the most saleable formats in television. "**

The format of a feature film being around 90 to 100 minutes, this obliged practically all the players in the game to change their prime-time format radically. They had to abolish the one-hour show and go for the 90-minute mini-series or television movie. Then, after the success of some counter-programming — and the commercial channels are usually very good at counter-programming — most of the public service channels were obliged to abandon even the mini-series and to use just the television series as the most flexible weapon to counter that counter-programming.

Today the result is that the television movie as a format is one of the most saleable, the most presentable, the most successful — at least for another couple of years I guess — formats in television, while the function of the long-running series was to block the audience. The audience loyalty which is normally established with a serial programme is used to counter the popularity of a big sporting event, if a rival channel has the sports event license. Another function is to plant an audience in the weakest point of the programme schedule in the hope that it will grow.

Prediction is difficult, but now I'll give you my personal view of the future. First of all TF1, Fininvest and Betataurus have recently acquired in an output deal all the rights over three years to whatever feature films come out of Hollywood. This means that the rest of the public service channels in Europe will no longer have feature films at their disposal as a form of competing with their commercial rivals. This, in a way, is the end of feature film programming for public service television. For example, ZDF, France and RAI will have only 25 feature films for the next year to programme. The rest are with their commercial competitors.

This means a big change in the programme schedule of all public service television in Europe, and it's a sort of coming back home. First they will have to re-establish the prime-time series show in order to block the audience at their highest possible point. Only by doing that can they try to counter the effect which a feature film normally has in a prime-time slot. Second, and this is already happening, in order to cover the same format (the 90-100 minute format) there will be an ever-increasing tendency to combine consecutive episodes of a one-hour series into a 90-minute segment.

This means they will buy only the serial type of series, not self-contained episodes because you cannot create one programme from two self-contained episodes. A third possibility is the creation of thematic nights, which means for instance that in the next season of Raidue, Friday night will be science fiction night and you'll have "**Space Rangers**", then after "**Space Rangers**", "**Star Trek IV**", and so on — the whole evening devoted to science fiction.

As far as content is concerned, this is of course the most difficult question. I don't know what will work, or won't work, in the future. I have some ideas, of course. To go back to the North-West Passage Theory, the public service broadcasters cannot abandon three segments of our market for ever, particularly if the commercial channels are tending to monopolise that biggest segment. So there is the route that Channel 4 took many years ago in Britain — to go for minorities. But, strictly speaking, that doesn't mean minorities, because a minority today in Europe might be 25 million Europeans, 9-12% of the European public who read the same literature, listen to the same music, watch the same movies, sometimes dress in the same fashions, but don't watch the same television. And this is an upmarket segment, maybe a future majority of that European nation.

Again, on content, we almost stopped making period drama in Europe in the '80s. The fashion in the '80s was to be contemporary, urban, young — or apparently young — highly motivated, individualistic and so on. I think we have now closed that era. Entering the end of this millennium will imply various things. It will imply what is happening already in America: I've seen pilots of two new series, both of them "coming back home" in a way, coming back to the little town, to the little family, rediscovering roots, forgetting about finance, forgetting cellular telephones and credit cards. I believe that this will be one of the prevailing trends in television series in the next five years.

> " *The general figures for co-production in Europe will decrease.* "

The second is the return of period drama. At the end of the millennium I guess we will, together with our public, reflect again on what the last thousand years was all about. Reflecting on that means new room for period drama, perhaps not as it was done in the past, perhaps from a very contemporary point of view, maybe a Roman empire series done in the style of "**Blade Runner**".

And what does this mean in terms of co-production? In one way, co-productions are going to decrease dramatically, but in another way they will increase. The sort of so-called exchange co-production will decrease because there is no longer the financial possibility of holding a stock of programmes which you cannot transmit because you're not totally convinced of their potential. So the general figures for co-production in Europe will decrease immensely. What kind of co-production will increase? I think that high production-value drama will maintain its share of the market. Crime and adventure stories are suitable for co-production, with strong above-the-line values, which means big casting, big directors, big writing.

What we will probably avoid in the future will be anthology series. This year might be the last year, I think, for this form of co-operation. Anthology series were series in which four or five countries each produced an episode, a television movie on one theme, let's say love stories. At the end of the day you pay for one and you have four or five or whatever. These have proved to be a complete flop. They don't work because it's a fantasy to hope to maintain a strong editorial line through all the episodes. I think that what I call 'blood and guns' is also on the decrease. We had enough of that in the '80s, plus there is now government concern about violence. I also believe that international sitcoms, as in the past, will not usually work.

To look on the positive side, I think we will have to devise more thematic, less generalised programmes to try to target our audience very clearly. This is a time of difference, this is a time of groups and it will be important to re-establish a loyal relationship between channel and audience. For too long, I guess under the pressure of competition, both public service and commercial television really didn't pay enough respect to their audience, they just tried to win the market in a sort of wild jungle. What has to be completely re-established is a very recognizable, identifiable relationship between channel, its editorial line, its choices, its tastes and the expectations of the public.

> " *For too long, I guess under the pressure of competition, both public service and commercial television really didn't pay enough respect to their audience.* "

Lastly, I'd like to mention some concerns about the future. I've read the figures for fiction production for the last three years and I have to say that I'm very concerned. In the last year, in Germany 1,080 hours of drama were produced; in the UK 1,200; in France 1,100; in Italy 750; in Spain 400. These are terrible figures, they mean that the demand for televised drama in Europe is five times what we can produce. It's depressing because the figures are no better this year than last year. It's a permanent crisis that's getting worse and worse year after year.

Most of our money is going to America in order to finance American programmes, American feature films. We are financing American talent — they are beautiful, and they know their job, but we are neglecting European talent, and not allowing it to grow up. So my final conclusion is that in the future we must campaign. I think that for the first time in my career I will ask for quotas. I was against them in the past. I was very much for a free market. This is the only way to enable our European audio-visual market to survive.

AUDIENCE RESEARCH

STEPHAN WARNIK

*Stephan Warnik was Head of Market Research and Programme Planning
at RTL4, Netherlands, and has recently been made responsible
for their new second channel.*

Whether you like it or not, Stephan Warnik began, it is the
ratings that decide the fate of a series. But if a series fails, you
should not blame the ratings, because the audience is never
wrong. If there is somebody to blame, it's likely to be the programme makers.

Warnik took RTL4 as his model, which he described as "a good
example of a commercial station in Europe." A member of the
CLT Group, RTL4 has been broadcasting in Holland since 1989.
Aimed primarily at a young audience, the station quickly became
market leader by poaching the biggest stars from public television.
RTL4 is now a broad family station with a market share of more
than 30% and an advertising share of almost 50%.

Warnik described RTL4's programme schedule, which, he said,
showed "the station's identity and what it stands for". The first
thing he pointed out was that the station had news, which gave it
an identity. "A station without any news has no face and will also
have a lot of problems with its identity." He also pointed to RTL4's
version of game show **"The Wheel of Fortune"**. "This means that
the station will probably be market leader, at least in that time-slot,
because all over the world this show has the highest market share."

Warnik pointed out the horizontal structure of the schedule, particularly between 6pm and 8pm. A schedule that is different for every day of the week would unsettle the audience, he said. He also drew attention to the US soap "**The Bold and the Beautiful**" as a sign that RTL4's audience was willing to accept foreign series, which does not happen in all European countries.

The choice of 7.30pm for the news slot was unusual. "News always starts at a round number — 8pm, 9pm, 10pm — so when it is at 7.30pm you know there must be a reason for this and that the reason will be counter-programming." The main news broadcast of the public station had been at 8pm for 30 years, so RTL4 decided to get its news broadcast in first. "The other possibility was to start half an hour after the public channel but late news is bad news." RTL4 was then free to schedule another programme against the other channel's news slot and for the last two years the channel has used a daily soap called "**Good Times Bad Times**". Another thing to look for in a schedule, he said, is the number of in-house programmes a channel has, because when a station has a lot of its own product it means that it profiles itself as a national station, as RTL4 does.

> " *But if a series fails, you should not blame the ratings, because the audience is never wrong.* "

On Monday, RTL4 schedules a programme originally based on the British series "**The Two of Us**", followed by a TV movie — a sign the station was aiming for a younger audience. On Tuesday, there is the game show "**Hitbingo**", which is aimed at an older audience. On Wednesday, a football night on other channels, there is "**Life Goes On**" and "**The Torkelsons**", which are programmes targeted at women. When the football ends after 10pm, RTL4 schedules a reality show called "**Ooggetuige**" (Eye Witness). Each night had a different target audience, something that advertisers like. On Sunday, for example, there is a foreign fiction line-up of "**Home Improvement**", "**Beverley Hills 90210**" and "**Fresh Prince**". "Which means that on that evening we are aiming at a young audience," he said.

Looking at the schedule as a whole, note the horizontal structure and the continuity in programme planning during the evenings; that when there is a programme for older people, it is followed by one aimed at the same audience. After 10 o'clock it changes. And when aiming for a young audience, the channel does so for the whole of that evening. A variety of evenings pleases advertisers, he repeated, who want to target different kinds of audiences.

Warnik then turned to the subject of audience research. Basically there are two different kinds of research — qualitative and quantitative. The former aims to answer the question: Why are people watching? This is very difficult to answer because it means getting into the minds of the audience, which means talking to them one by one or in a very small group, which is very expensive. It is too difficult to get large enough numbers for the results to be reliable.

> " *Basically there are two different kinds of research — qualitative and quantitative. The former aims to answer the question: Why are people watching?* "

The qualitative techniques in common use are the individual questionnaire or the group questionnaire. Researchers use different tools to help people explain what they do and do not like. "You can give a person a vote or ask what he thinks about this picture, or you can let them watch a pilot." Another problem with qualitative research is that it cannot be compared with other surveys — each study is unique. A very experienced researcher should be used, otherwise the results can be almost meaningless.

In some cases researchers will use devices that track the movement of the eye or measure the amount of sweat released while watching a programme. "The advantage of these techniques is that they cannot lie. People can lie to you when you are talking to them but the body cannot."

The most common type of qualitative research is known in the Netherlands as "Q Vision". A group of around eight people are given a box with a handle. They push the handle forward when the see something they like and pull it back when they don't. Their answers are processed by a computer so that the producer or the scriptwriter get instant feedback as the programme is being shown.

After the test viewers can be asked why they liked or disliked certain sections. It is also possible to interrupt the viewing to ask questions, which has the advantage of not giving the people time to forget. Another advantage over group discussions is that people are not influenced by what others say. Qualitative research is also used for testing the image and position of the channel, or for testing programme presenters, scripts and pilots.

Quantitative research, on the other hand, aims to answer the question: How many people are watching? This can be done on an *ad hoc* basis or using a panel which gives continuous input. An example of *ad hoc* research is asking 600 people whether or not they think Clinton should resign. However, a panel is more commonly used in television.

Some years ago, a viewing panel of about 1000 people were given a diary to fill in every evening. They were supposed to record what they watched in every quarter hour, but what people wrote proved to be unreliable. More common in Europe now is the people-meter, which started about ten years ago. It is a electronic device that records what programmes a person watches.

Interactive television offers the possibility for instant ratings. "This would be a dream for me, but probably a nightmare for scriptwriters," Warnik said. During or after a soap, for example, people could be asked if they thought a certain character should be punished, killed or praised. The scriptwriters will then have the chance to mould the script to suit the wishes of the audience. "I wouldn't be surprised if one day producers let the audience write the script, or lead it in a certain direction." In Brazil panels of 100 or 200 housewives are asked which characters in a telenovela they like most. The most popular get more airtime and very quickly because the lead time is very short.

Television channels don't get instant ratings with the people-meter, but they see the figures the next morning. Depending on the size of the country, between 1,000 and 1,500 households have a small computer connected to the television which knows when a particular member of the family starts to watch and what they are watching. As all the family are registered, the social class, age, etc. of each person is also available. The information is sent over the phone lines at night to a central computer which then calculates all the ratings in time for the next morning.

Warnik then explained the key terms. "Ratings" means the size of a TV audience, usually expressed as a percentage of the total possible audience. So for the Netherlands, with 13.5 million people, a rating of 1% represents 135,000 viewers. In the US they distinguish between people ratings and household ratings. Household ratings were not as precise, because an unspecified number of people could be watching.

Another important key term is "share" — the percentage of the maximum TV audience in a given area that is watching television at a specific time. So when 30% of the population is watching at a certain time, the total audience is 30%. A programme with a rating of 6%, is therefore being watched by 20% of all available viewers at that moment. Share can also be expressed as a percentage of a specific target group — i.e. 30% of housewives. It is easy to get a 50% market share in the afternoon but it's very difficult to do in prime time because the competition is much tougher.

> " "Ratings" means the size of a TV audience, usually expressed as a percentage of the total possible audience. "

"**The Wheel of Fortune**", shown at 7pm, gets a rating of 7%, or 950,000 viewers, which equals a market share of almost 40%. Broadcast at 11.30pm, "**Columbo**" gets a rating of 7.1%, but because more people are watching in the evening than in the afternoon, the market share is 10% lower than "**The Wheel of Fortune**". At 00.45pm, "**Oprah Winfrey**" has a rating of 2.4%, but has a market share of 46.9% because there is no competition late in the evening. To estimate whether a programme performs well or not, you must always look first at the ratings, then at the market share, then at the time slot and compare your results with other programmes on at the same time.

Another important indicator is the "inheritance figure", which is how many people watched a certain programme as a percentage of the number of people who watched the programme before it. The higher this percentage the better. "You can see whether or not two programmes are linked together well and whether or not the audience flows through your whole programme schedule in a good way. A low inheritance figure means you have a switch of audience at that moment and you must ask yourself whether or not you must change the order of the programmes."

All this information gives the scheduler an impression of the viewing behaviour of the people. It shows when people watch, what they watch, how long they watch for, and how viewing is spread throughout the day. These detailed figures also show that different programmes have different profiles. It shows which are the favourite programmes and what zapping behaviour looks like in a graph. Looking at the ratings every day give you an understanding of what an audience likes and what can be done to change programming to suit their tastes.

Viewing patterns change during the year. In December and January the total ratings are the highest. When the sun starts to shine, people watch less television. This is made worse because many broadcasters offer a weaker schedule in the summer and many repeats. RTL4 continues strong programming in the summer knowing the competition would be weak and that people would still be watching. The channel chose to launch "**Beverley Hills 9210**" in May when it was the only new programme on Dutch television. It subsequently got a lot of attention in the newspapers and the good weather fitted with the California lifestyle of the programme.

RTL4 begins its winter season in September to get their new programmes on the air before the other channels. And when the other channels plan a major launch, RTL4 will schedule a Bond movie or something like it to try to "kill" the programme. The biggest difference between winter and summer time falls between 5pm and 8pm, because people want to stay outside when the weather is fine. There is not much difference after 10pm so programmes can be swapped from summer to winter without much problem.

In considering demographics, the most important factor is age. For example, in the 13-19 year age category, "**The Bold and The Beautiful**" scored the highest rating for the early evening. But this changes the moment "**The Wheel of Fortune**" starts, which is popular with a much older audience. The older audience — people of 50 years and older — tend to have the highest ratings, at least until 8pm, because they are such a large group. The very young — 6 to 12 years old — tend to be in bed after 8pm, which accentuates the tendency that the older people are, the higher the ratings are.

"I want to emphasise that when you write for a programme that will be scheduled at 7pm, you must realise that about 62% of your potential audience is more than 35 years old. A lot of the scripts I see are aiming at an upmarket audience or people aged between 20 or 34. It's very dangerous to schedule a programme like that before 8.30pm. Scriptwriters," Warnik concluded, "should know what time their programme is scheduled for and what the potential audience is."

" When you write for a programme that will be scheduled at 7pm, you must realise that about 62% of your potential audience is more than 35 years old. "

There are important differences in the viewing patterns of men and women. In Holland at least, women tend to watch more television than men with the biggest gap at 5pm and between 8pm and 10pm. At 5pm some 60% of the audience is female. The only time that men watch more television is after 11 pm. "I'm not sure whether or not this is the case in all European countries. For example, television in southern Europe tends to have two primetimes — between noon and 2pm and then at 10pm when everyone comes home."

Social class is also an indicator of different viewing habits. In Holland, the lower-ranked groups tend to watch more television, particularly in the early evenings. But after 10pm, the difference is not so marked. "When you have a programme aimed at the higher social classes it is pointless starting at 7pm."

In Holland, of the top 50 programmes in the ratings only eight are drama or comedies and the first-placed one ranks number 21. Around 19 are game shows and some 23 are sports or news or current affairs programmes. Sports programmes tend to get the highest ratings, but this is not always the case throughout Europe. In the UK, for example, the highest-rating programmes are soap operas.

Scriptwriters should bear in mind that the ratings and viewing data are not set in stone and can change. "You should also take notice of the target group you are writing for, and when this target group is watching. And you must also take notice of your lead-in programme because people are in a different mood when they come out of "**The Cosby Show**" than when they come out of a programme like "**Twin Peaks**". The kind of lead-in programme can dicatate the sort of people that will be watching and what kind of mood they'll be in." This information may not be available when writing the first scripts, but once the programme is on the air, writers should look to see whether or not the target audience is being reached and whether or not the ratings or market shares are increasing or decreasing and whether they are doing so for the specific target audience.

(This is a summary of the lecture.)

DEVELOPMENT OF A NEW SITCOM INTO A LONG-RUNNING SERIES

HUMPHREY BARCLAY

Prolific and innovative producer of situation comedy and
ex Head of Light Entertainment at London Weekend Television,
now running Humphrey Barclay Productions.
Has won many national and international awards.

The series "**Desmond's**" came about because a Commissioning Editor at Channel 4, the UK's cultural and minority interest channel, said to Humphrey Barclay one day, "Nobody has brought me a new black situation comedy." Barclay then set about finding a black writer to develop an idea, which was not easy because there were very few black writers working in television in the UK. He contacted a writer, recent winner of a Channel 4 prize, who presented the idea of a sitcom set in a barber's shop. Barclay said, "My heart sank straight away because I'd seen half a dozen pilots set in English hairdressers which are full of camp young men and women with blue hair, and you're falling asleep quicker than the people in the chairs." But the writer explained that a West Indian barber shop is very different, a community place where people drop in and spend the whole day. This is what Barclay had been looking for, "a forum, a location into which the comedy comes". The idea was for a workplace with a resident family and a team of regular, amusing characters.

The pilot episode was screened and Humphrey Barclay pointed out how hard the team had worked to create positive images of black people, something which seemed slightly overdone in retrospect. One of the main strengths of the series, he believes, was the central relationship between the husband and wife. Another aspect the team had worked hard at was to show that black people do not all come from the West Indies. The Commissioning Editor was pleased with the first episode but pointed out that the series was almost timeless. He suggested the creation of a yuppie character to suit the reality of the late 1980's in the UK. The character they created was the bank manager son of the main character, who has a bad relationship with his father — giving rise to conflict and humour.

> " *...the relationships and problems are universal, which has given the show a broad appeal beyond the target audience.* "

Having described the series and its creation, Humphrey Barclay pointed out that although more than 70 episodes had been commissioned, the show was not a 'world seller', despite being sold to the USA. It was originally created for a minority audience, but the family element, the relationships and problems are universal, which has given the show a broad appeal beyond the target audience. The characters, young and old, male and female, gave many different "points of access" to the audience.

After twenty episodes, the originating writer asked for help and Barclay was able to bring in other writers and build a team — "which in my experience has always enriched a programme a great deal," he said. The six new members of the team, all black and from very different backgrounds, were not experienced sitcom writers. "I have always gone on the belief that I can teach them the craft if they have got the inspiration."

The team meets at the beginning of each series to discuss its direction, specific story-lines and to pool ideas. Individual writers are then given a storyline that appeals to them, which they then work on with the script editor or producer (Barclay), before returning to the group to develop them further. The writers then write their episodes individually, often many drafts. "I don't let writers send me scripts — they have to bring them. I clear the whole day and I sit and read the script there and then and immediately sit down and work through it with them." The process applies for every draft. The advantages of reading through the script with the writer were, he said, the savings in time, the potential to bring out things that neither individual might have thought of, and as a way of keeping the writer in good spirits. "Even if the writer has brought me a script that's produced the longest face in me, by the time he goes away I make sure he's up again and knows what to do next."

Once they are well developed, the next stage of the process is a team revision of the scripts, sometimes preceded by a read-though by the cast. In the team revision, the scripts are gone through line by line. "Sometimes we will actually re-write a scene as a team round the table... every line is challenged, and the multiple voices and suggestions that we get into the episode makes it far richer than it would have been in the first place."

One of the pitfalls that Humphrey Barclay identified, particularly when a new writer joins a team, is the temptation to introduce new characters. He realised this was a mistake, because if you want to do a particular story it should be given to one of the regular characters, who are already known and liked by the audience. "To concentrate on the established characters is very important, for the satisfaction of the viewer and the happiness of the actors." Another realisation was the need to remember the focus of the series, in this case Desmond. "We have to make sure that every story eventually affects, or is affected by, Desmond... Focus on the strengths of the character and of the series. Continually remind yourself what the series is about."

> " *Even if the writer has brought me a script that's produced the longest face in me, by the time he goes away I make sure he's up again and knows what to do next.* "

Finally, Barclay talked about pay. The Writers Guild minimum rate for a half hour sitcom is around £2,500 for one transmission. The Desmond's team are generally on £3,500, while more experienced writers can command £6,000 a script and really exceptional ones £10,000. In his team system, half is paid on commission, a quarter on delivery of a finished script and the last quarter when he is happy with it.

(This is a summary of the lecture.)

THE DESTINY OF A TV SERIES

RIFT FOURNIER

Rift Fournier is a scriptwriter. He has spent over thirty years writing for television in the USA, and moved to Barcelona while writing "Dark Justice" for Lorimar/TV3. He now lives in LA.

The writer of some 300 episodes for US series, from "**Kojak**" to "**Highway to Heaven**", Rift Fournier began his talk with an attention-grabbing yell. He introduced himself, describing some of the series he has worked on, before moving on to his main theme, which was characters.

"What we are talking about is something really simple, and I want to read something to you: "They are good, they are bad, they are weak, they are strong, they are wise, they are foolish. So am I." That's what character is, he said, and one of the most frequent problems writers encounter is creating characters with dimensions. "I happen to believe that the destiny of any television series is based on the moral strength of the principal character or characters."

There is a big difference, he said, between the kind of characters that work for film, plays and novels and the characters that work for television. "The people we invite into our homes every day or every week are people we have to like and we have to trust. And that's why it is important to make these characters with something of ourselves in them."

According to Fournier, television shows can't deal with the larger-than-life characters that Arnold Shwarzenegger plays, characters whose persona's are too big for the small screen. "So you must create characters who are just a little bit larger than life, which makes them interesting, but not overwhelming — if a character overwhelms you, you won't invite him back into your house."

He showed a clip from the series "**Kojak**" to illustrate some of the points. "The show was always doing this human theatre. It was always about Kojak's relationships. He always created a family in each show. Solving the crime was secondary." Audiences today have become bored with all-action crime-solving, and expect some "humanity" from their characters. This applies to sit-coms as well as drama series. He cited the character of Archie Bunker in the series "**All In The Family**" as an example. "This guy was so tough and so wonderful and so dumb and we loved him...everybody knew that behind all that stuff that Archie used to do, he was not a bad guy."

> " *The people we invite into our homes every day or every week are people we have to like and we have to trust.* "

Fournier then showed a clip from the US series "**NYPD Blues**" in which the two principal characters were introduced. One of the characters, Sipowicz, ends up being shot, for reasons of his own inner weaknesses. "These weren't crime stories in the traditional sense, but arise out of character defects, out of the weakness of these principal characters. The story was generated from within the characters."

"In the early days of cop shows, the characters would spend a lot of time chasing the criminals, with the audience certain that the bad guys would be caught. Well in this new show, we don't give a shit about the bad guy. What we care about is the relationship between the good guys."

He made the point that in America, TV evolved to create shared communities of stories and characters for people living in suburban isolation. "In these new suburbs there was no street life, and so at night everybody, instead of going out into the street and talking with their neighbours, sat down in front of the television. And these characters started coming into their lives." In television, the plot was only important as a vehicle for discovering more about the characters.

Fournier showed a clip from the US series "**Magnum**", which ran for seven years based, he said, on essentially one story-line. "There's a saying in America: 'No good deed goes unpunished.' Well, "**Magnum**" was on television for seven years based on that joke, because every time he did something for somebody something crazy would happen. But the audiences really liked "**Magnum**" because he was one of these guys who got through all the craziness of life and kept smiling — he was an optimist." "**The Fugitive**" was another series that relied on the character who "in every story would stop and be a human being. That's why audiences loved that show — it was about his humanity." "**Hawaii Five-O**", on the other hand, had no such human characters and relied on palm-trees and girls to keep the audiences happy.

"**Cagney and Lacey**" was another successful series which focused on relationships and character. "They were not perfect women... they fought like hell, one of them was married, she had fights with her husband. The series explored everything that you could imagine about women, every issue came up in that show." "**MASH**" was another example. "It wasn't about surgery, it was about the relationships of those guys. And from their characters, each week, came the story. They were able to keep us liking them, every week, year after year, for eleven years."

> *" In television, the plot was only important as a vehicle for discovering more about the characters. "*

Rift Fournier revealed some of the techniques he uses when creating characters. "If you want to create a character, let's say it's a cop, I'd imagine I was a journalist and I'd sit down and interview him, create a whole big inventory of questions. But I wouldn't interview him about being a cop, I'd interview him about being a human being. If you decide he's married, talk to him about his wife... the emotional inventory of this character." Another technique was to close your eyes and imagine that this character is in the room, and you find out things about them just by looking at them. "Also, I think every character has to have a secret, one we never find out, an emotional secret, it's the motor that drives the character. You, the writer know it, but you never share it with the audience."

Fournier discussed casting and its effect on a series. He cited the series "**Police Woman**". "They had a male actor who was going to be the star of the show and they got Angie Dickinson to play the second lead, but it was really to be a male-dominated show. They did the first three episodes and Angie Dickinson blew him off the screen, she was so good, so human. And suddenly it was her show. No matter how wonderfully we create these characters, we ain't the bosses." Rift advocated that Europe's writers should become writer-producers. "It's the only way you'll protect your work, by protecting the characters and casting your vision."

In conclusion, Fournier said: "You can take every Emmy-winning episode in American television in the last fifteen years, you can ask the audiences, you can ask anybody in the business, if they can remember what the plots were and they'll look at you with a blank stare. They don't care about the plots. They care about the people."

(This is a summary of the lecture.)

THE NARRATIVE STRUCTURE OF DRAMA

JEANNE GLYNN

Jeanne Glynn was a writer on the daytime series "General Hospital" for four years, and also worked on "All My Children" and "Search for Tomorrow". She is currently writing the screenplay for a CBS serial, "Guiding Light".

Jeanne Glynn began with a brief history of television serials, or 'soap operas', in America, from their origins in radio series in the 1940s to the landmark series "**General Hospital**", which went on the air in 1963 and has been running ever since. The most important elements, according to the originators of "**General Hospital**", were character, consistency and credibility. Glynn has now added to that wisdom: "Character, craving, conflict, commitment are what, in retrospect, I think one needs."

As a writer, Jeanne Glynn started out on the series "**All My Children**", before moving to "**General Hospital**". She described the script-writing process. "On this show, as in many, head-writers would do the bible, or long-term story; associate head-writers, would do the 'weekly thrust' — the narrative of what part of the story will be done that week; breakdown writers, normally five of them, would take the thrust and break it down into five days, each of about 22 scenes, with 7 full sets, plus the number of characters needed for each day."

The breakdown writers and head writer would meet on Monday to determine which story points to cover. By Tuesday work would begin on the breakdown, which was reviewed on Wednesday, returned for revisions on Friday, then back to the head writer and producer for their approval, before being passed to the script writer who had less than a week to get the completed script back. "Of necessity, time and organisation are paramount, as everyone is dependent on everyone else. On a good daytime series, normally everything runs six weeks ahead of airing."

Jeanne Glynn then turned to the structure of the one-hour script. A careful breakdown of the story was essential, she said. "It may be a painful and slow process, but is saves so much time in the scripting process if any holes are found early on." The basic script is made up of six acts with an A story (the main one that carries the day), a B story (which carries through to the next day), and a C story (an attention-grabbing story to draw the audience). "The teaser, the opening, is often the C story, with the episode building up to the strongest, thus the order being C, B, A."

> *" The most formidable thing is to work out how to take the central idea and carry it through 22 interesting scenes. "*

The teaser runs until the first commercial break, then Act 1 and the main characters leading to the A story. "The most formidable thing is to work out how to take the central idea and carry it through 22 interesting scenes. It is demanding but necessary to plan the show around this formula, although many writers will say they don't have the time, but it is where the weaknesses show up." She admitted that the process sounds very mechanical when compared to the European way — "but in America it works for this genre", she said, especially when you're turning out 5 hours of story each week.

It is Glynn's belief that the actors carry the audience, while the writer helps make the characters popular by structuring the story. She described it as: "Moving through the acts, but ending by not satisfying the audience, giving so much but holding back a certain amount." In every scene, she said, there must be one character that the audience is interested in and can identify with. "Characters, to be successful, need to crave something — sex, money, status, marriage — a drive towards something. There must be conflict, which is something the audience needs to see in the first minute or so. And the character must stay committed to himself or herself, just as the writers must remain committed to their creations."

The 'job' of the show is to engage the audience's emotions, she said. "Whatever you are writing about, there must be an emotional thread. There is love and hate and a scale with indifference right in the middle. That point of indifference is the one where the audience will turn off." If the series wants to deal with serious issues, the message must appear as subtext not as propaganda. In 1984 the daytime soap **"Search for Tomorrow"** portrayed date rape for the first time. "After it was broadcast we received more letters from women who had gone through what had been shown than had been received throughout all the previous 15 years of the programme. So I emphasise, we must play, not say — show rather than preach."

> *" In every scene there must be one character that the audience is interested in and can identify with. "*

In each of the 22 scenes there will be certain elements, she said. "Each good scene will contain attitude, action, subtext and story points." She gave an example of a 'teaser' breakdown of a typical 'morning-after' scene. "Mary's kitchen (location), 8 am (the time affects props, lighting, costume). Mary is furious (attitude), she has found out that her husband has been unfaithful (subtext)." The action would depend on the genre — "in comedy she would put her husband's ties in the blender, present him with an inedible breakfast", whereas in a dramatic series the action would be "heavy drama".

"If you, as a writer, try to fill a pause with feeling, rather than dialogue, you should always remember that an audience's attention span is very short, so several emotional actions must be contained in the pause. You must also be very clear as to whom the story belongs — who the protagonist is in each particular scene." Serial storytelling is an art as well as a craft, and each successful series develops its own personality, pace, and point of view".

(This is a summary of the lecture.)

ADAPTING BOOKS FOR TELEVISION

ADRIAN HODGES

From reporter for Screen International, Acquisitions Executive at Thorn EMI Screen Entertainment, Head of Development at the National Film Development Fund, Adrian Hodges has been a full time TV and film screen-writer since 1990.

Adrian Hodges began by asking "What kind of books make good television?" He answered this by analysing what books do best and what television does best.

Books, he said, are an imaginative medium, the reader has a unique relationship with the novelist and the characters. TV, however, is a literal medium, imposing an image of the character on the viewer. Books can explore the inner life of the characters, whereas TV, in general, cannot. Books can take their time to make a point, while TV depends on pace, plots, action and incident. Books are invariably longer than TV scripts. Books can have several points of view, whereas in most cases TV drama is told with the camera as a neutral, objective observer. Great TV depends on characters, whereas good books can get away with a lot of plot. Books can be read very quickly, with vast amounts of information absorbed from every page. In TV, every detail requires a camera set-up, it is a more painstaking medium.

With the above in mind, the first step in adaptation is choosing the book. It is important to find the right book. Common mistakes include thinking: a successful book will automatically make good TV; that classic novels make classic TV; that glossy, all-action 'airport' novels make great TV; that the 'best', or most literary novels, should make good TV.

What does the writer who adapts a book actually do? He changes things. No book can go straight onto the screen. There are no rules, he said, every writer must find his or her own approach. But certain vital questions need to be answered before beginning.

Do I adapt a book I don't like? Loving a novel can be a handicap, so can hating it, but at some level you have to respect it. You should not adapt a work if you want to subvert what the author intended. But if you believe that what you are doing is in the spirit of the work and follows the author's intentions, you can take as many liberties as you want. Should I have a relationship with the original author? Almost certainly not. If you seek guidance, approval or friendship, you will almost certainly be inhibited.

> " What does the writer who adapts a book actually do? He changes things. No book can go straight onto the screen. "

According to Adrian Hodges, the first rule of adaptation is that nothing is sacred. "A friend of mine referred to adaptation as tearing the book to pieces, throwing the pages up in the air, and seeing where they land. I know what he meant." It is almost certain that the structure of a TV series will need to be different to that of the book. Structure may not be of paramount importance in a novel, but in a TV series it is essential. The job of the adaptor is to bring vital character and action to the foreground and to minimise and discard all that isn't as relevant.

We are all used to the idea that a 500 page book can be turned into a 90 minute film. This cannot be achieved without throwing a great deal out. There is more time available in a TV series, but it does not necessarily mean you can put more of the novel in. It could make the series intolerably slow. "Successful TV", Adrian Hodges said, "depends on making the audience feel that a great deal is going on. But the mere accumulation of events is not quite the same as this. Audiences rapidly become bored and restless if presented with action pure and simple. A very few dramatic incidents can make for a highly stimulating hour's television, provided the audience can become intimately involved with the life of the characters."

One of the key tasks is deciding what goes and what stays. You may have to drop someone from the book because they don't fit your proposed structure. What will the effect of this be? Is the point of view the right one?

TV needs to establish its main characters and plots very quickly. "In my view, you are more aware of time passing on TV than in any other medium." It is very important that the principal characters are established early and that they hold the centre of the drama. Which leads to the question of structure. Is the structure of the book right for your series? In most cases the answer is no. The first thing the adaptor must do is to decide how to bring the main characters to the fore and to keep them at the centre of the action. This inevitably has an impact on the structure — remember, don't be afraid to make radical changes.

"In my view, the adaptation of a book to TV inevitably involves a process of simplification. This doesn't mean that the TV version need be less intelligent or less challenging, but it does mean that it will usually be more linear, more focused and less inclined to wander..."

Another problem facing the adaptor is the author's voice, something which readers like about books and hope to see in the TV series. Failure to catch the 'tone' of a book can lead a series to fail. The problem can be solved in several ways. Voice-over is one option, but is often not suitable. Characters can talk to camera, but this is very risky. The most common solution is to work the author's voice into the dialogue and action of the characters. In some situations this means thinking up dialogue which conveys the same spirit as the author's descriptions. Which begs the question: how much of his own voice should an adaptor use? "That's easy. As much as he needs to. Very often a skilled TV adpator writes better dialogue than a novelist."

Dialogue in novels, no matter how witty, often falls flat when transferred to a TV script. Why? Because it can take too long. Dialogue on the page can be read swiftly and is often highly stylised, i.e. not as people speak. Over-long speeches are the curse of TV adaptations. "On the page we concentrate solely on the words, but on TV we become acutely conscious that an actor is going on for a long time." This is partly because TV is a realistic medium and we expect it to be true to life. TV dialogue does not exactly mirror life, but tends to be snappier, shorter and more directly focused. A long speech is reserved for an important moment in the drama.

To summarise, the fundamentals of a good adaptation are character, structure, action and dialogue in that order. Good adaptation involves re-writing the novel. The adaptor owes nothing to the original except respect for its intentions — but this does not justify change for its own sake.

> " *Good adaptation involves re-writing the novel. The adaptor owes nothing to the original except respect for its intentions.* "

Finally, extracts of "**Tales of the City**" were shown to illustrate the comments made above. Adrian Hodges pointed out several risks involved in the project: the books are very well-known, the author is still alive, and the readers of the novels feel passionately about them. Instead of tearing the books up and starting again, the screen-writer has, in this case, been very faithful to the original. The structure is nearly identical to the books, the dialogue is almost verbatim — short, punchy and dramatic. The style of the book is episodic, with a multi-character format — i.e. no leading character.

"In conclusion it seems to me that is some ways books make less good television series than original ideas, but that doesn't alter the fact that books have been and remain a staple of television entertainment."

(This is a summary of the lecture.)

OTHER TALKS

Finally, we would like to mention the participation of the other professionals who spoke during the PILOTS workshops. Their words have not been published or summarised for a variety of reasons. In some cases, the lectures were tied in with the screening of episodes or clips in such a way that they would not make sense to a reader who did not attend. In other cases, the topic of the lecture was considered too specific to be relevant to the broader audience this book is targeted at. On behalf of the participants who benefited from their contributions, PILOTS would like to thank the following:

Anat Birnbaum of French pay-TV channel Canal+, spoke on the broadcaster's formula for success, its rapidly diversifying activities and the opportunities it presented as a source of financing.

Anat Birnbaum started her media career with the BBC World Service, moving to Tele Hachette in France, where she was appointed to head the Distribution Department. In 1983 she joined the Canal Plus project, where she now heads the TV fiction acquisitions department.

Clive Brill of the BBC drama series department spoke on the all-important first five minutes of a pilot episode, about how to grab the audience's attention. He illustrated his lecture with clips from **"Casualty"** and other British series.

Having worked on "The Archers" and "Citizens", Clive Brill joined BBC Radio as commissioning editor for Series and Serials. He moved to the TV drama series department where he was responsible for the recruiting and training of script editors and is now producing for BBC TV.

Doc Comparato, the scriptwriter and creator behind many of Latin America's most successful drama series, replied to previous lectures on adaptation, characters, dramatic construction and writing methods in Europe. He also discussed the sources of creative ideas.

Doc Comparato is a Brazilian scriptwriter and script editor, living in Portugal. He has written series for RAI/Globo, and in collaboration with Gabriel García Márquez, for TVE. He co-scripted the latest major series for Catalan television, "Arnau".

Jean Pierre Dusseaux, a Director of Development for an independent production company, discussed the relationship between audience behaviour patterns and programme scheduling.

Since 1982, Jean Pierre Dusseaux has worked in French television for FR3 and Antenne 2, in the areas of development and programming, as well as for the INA and RTL Radio.

Fernando Labrada, General Manager of PILOTS' principal sponsor the Media Business School, described another of the programme's initiatives, a joint investigation with the European Broadcasting Union into public and private television in Europe.

During his career with RTVE, Fernando Labrada held a number of positions, notably Director of Production Services and Director of the Documentation Centre. He was General Manager of Radio and Television in the Olympic Stadium during the 1992 Olympic Games, and is currently General Manager of the Media Business School.

Gudie Lawaetz, former General Manager of the Media Business School (MBS), described the workings of the TV Business School, a programme complementary to PILOTS aimed at producers, which she set up.

Gudie Lawaetz's career in television included directing and producing. She subsequently held the position of General Manager of the Media Business School in Madrid, until late 1992. Her presence at PILOTS was as Director of the Television Business School in Lubeck.

Pascal Lonhay, scriptwriter and producer. Using the film "**The Apartment**" and the US series "**Alf**", he described the workings of the three act structure and narrative structure.

*Pascal Lonhay has wide experience in writing, script editing, and doctoring for both television and cinema, including "**Toto Le Heros**", "**The Royal Game**". Script consultant for Eave, he has written the new Jaco Van Dormael feature film.***Poul Malmkjaer,** a commissioning editor for mini-series for Denmark's public television channel, spoke on the principles of dramatic tension, under the headline: "Show the Banana Peel".

Poul Malmkjaer has worked for the Drama Department of Danmarks Radio-Tv for over 30 years, as Head of Acquisitions, Commissioning Editor and Script Editor of the series "The Weekly".

Renate Roginas, a producer with the French production company TelFrance, described her experience of French-German co-productions, with particular emphasis on the new series "**Fire and Flame**".

Having worked for over 13 years with TelFrance, during which she has made some 350 hours of programming, Renate Roginas has made French-German co-production her speciality. The latest success is "Fire and Flame", (with a German partner and France 3 providing technical support) currently showing in Germany and France.

Christian Routh, Selection Coordinator at the European Script Fund, spoke about the Incentive Funding scheme, whereby producers were given more substantial loans to develop several projects.

Prior to joining the ESF Christian Routh was a development executive at Canon and Red Rooster.

PROJECTS FROM 1993

POBLE NOU

Josep Maria Benet i Jornet, Gisela Pou, Enric Gomà
Televisió de Catalunya
Sant Joan Despí 08080 Barcelona, Spain
Tel: 34 3 499 9561 Fax: 34 3 473 1322
130 x 30'
Daily soap/Drama

Synopsis

The setting of this series is Poble Nou, the Olympic Village built for the 1992 Games in Barcelona. What is left of the original, down-market area now borders on a modern district of high-technology buildings, peaceful green zones and a predominantly Yuppie population. The conflict arises from the clash of two worlds, which meet in the supermarket on the border of the old part and the new. The shop has been built on the site of an old *bodega*, with the winnings of the lottery, and it is the focus of the comings and goings of the neighbourhood. All of the traditional elements of a daily soap are incorporated: infidelities, illegitimacy, homosexuality, the generation gap, truancy, petty crime, unemployment, prostitution. The main characters are the couple who run the supermarket and have a new flat in the Olympic Village, their three children, and their relatives and friends.

Current situation

Production started preparation in August 1993. In October, work started on the studio sets, and test-shooting began in November. By early January, 5 episodes were being produced every 6 days. The one-hour pilot episode was transmitted on 10th January during prime time, and the series has run since then on a daily basis and with a weekend repetition, on the main Catalan channel. On transmission of episode 40, in early March, there were still twenty finished episodes in hand, with a further 35 completed scripts. The ratings are very satisfactory and, because of the nature of the production schedule, small but essential changes can be introduced at the last moment depending on audience reaction.

LOGGERHEADS

Ralph Christians, Agust Gudmunsson, Bernhard Koellisch
Magmafilm Iceland
Gamli Alafoss, 270 Mosfellsborg, Iceland
Tel: 354 1 668008 Fax: 354 1 668009
13 x 25'
Sitcom/comedy

Synopsis

The Vikings have had a bad press. For too long they have been mis-represented as blond, blue-eyed maniacs interested only in pillage and rape. "**Loggerheads**" aims to set the record straight, with a rough, rude period-piece about fairly civilised life on the fjord. The story begins nearly 1000 years ago, as Christianity first reaches Iceland. The story centres on two families, a "nouveau riche" Christian family and a traditional "berserker" family and the running disputes they have with each other and with the chief of the village. The cast is made up of stolen princesses and slaves from all over Europe. The team behind Loggerheads describe the series as: '"**Asterix**" meets "**Monty Python**" meets "'**Allo 'Allo**" meets "**The Flinstones**"'.

Current situation

The team came to the first workshop with storylines, character des-criptions and drawings showing the visual approach, and the backing of the European Script Fund. They benefitted greatly from the workshops, improving and extending the scripts, and obtaining another development grant from the Nordic Film & TV Fund, and a cooperation agreement signed with NDF Germany. During the second workshop, further development support was promised by the ECA (RAI, Channel 4, ZDF). The production schedule plans six finished scripts by the end March 1994, and, depending on negotia-tions for a production-contract with the ECA, could go into pre-pro-duction in May 1994, with the first day of shooting scheduled for the end of the year, probably in Ireland.

KLINKEVALS (THE TWO PENNY DANCE)

Jane Aamund, Per Holst, Mogens Klovedal
Per Holst Film
Rentemestervej 69A, DK-2400 Copenhagen NV, Denmark
Tel: 45 38 887800 Fax: 45 38 887878
6 x 50'
Drama serial/comedy

Synopsis

This television series is based on the best-selling novels of the same name, written by Jane Aamund. The saga begins in 1880's Copenhagen, in the poorest, most colourful quarter of the city, built during the reign of King Christian IV. Here, working-class families lived in small apartments in six-storey buildings and the landscape of the streets was a mixture of apartment blocks and small one-family houses. This is an epic story which follows the Jensen family — particularly Juliane Jensen, a single parent — through pain and happiness, the birth and death of children, marriages and divorces, spanning half a century from 1880 until 1930, when Copenhagen was in the throes of the Great War.

Current situation

German co-producers, Metropolis Filmproduktion, have shown great interest in the series, and the team expects to be able to either co-produce or place a considerable part of the actual production work with Defa Studios (Babelsberg) in Berlin. They expect support from the Berlin and Brandenburg Film Assistance Program and hope to attract interest from a major German tv-producer. Danish TV2 and Swedish Television 1 (Drama) are also very positive and the Norwegian Norsk Rikskringkasting is also expected to become involved. Completion of the scripts is progressing well and on schedule.

MONKEYS

Laurence Bowen, Dom Shaw, Matthew Bird, Philip Clarke,
Brian McGill
Diverse Productions/BBC Television
Gorleston Street, London W14 8XS, UK
Tel: 44 71 603 4567 Fax: 44 71 603 2148
13 x 50'
Drama series/Drama

Synopsis

Europe, and Britain in particular, are both blessed and cursed with the best and the worst press in the world. The pioneering work of photo-journalists is surpassed only by the excesses of the paparazzi, the former with their desire to expose corruption, to seek the truth, and the latter with their voracious appetite for sex, sleaze and scandal. To be a 'monkey' or a 'snapper' is, for many, to be in the frontline. The sheer adrenalin of the work — the chase, the danger, the fun of it — is, however, constantly undermined by moral uncertainty. The 'Nikon chorus' can reflect or distort as easily as any editorial. The snappers must travel the ragged line of compromise between truth and untruth. This series reveals the diverse, outrageous and extraordinary world of press photography, from the premises of the GPP, Global Photo Press, agency in London.

Current situation

The team worked and reworked the material brought to the first workshop, and currently have a revised second draft of the second episode and a further six storylines, and consider the package finished. They are concluding a theoretical casting in order to present to the Controller at the BBC in April.

FREUNDE (FRIENDS)

Karl Heinz Willschrei, Richard Reitinger
Borussia Media Produktions
Verlängerte Daumstrasse 16, W-1000 Berlin 20, Germany
Tel: 49 30 334 1031 Fax: 49 30 334 0514
26 x 60'
Drama series/Drama

Synopsis

This project is a new type of family series for Germany. Not father-mother-child stories but serial portraits of a circle of friends who are entangled in each other's lives. Singles, married and unmarried couples, with and without children. It is set in the Germany of the '90s and its protagonists are all thirtyish, and belong to the successful academic middle-class, trendsetters with reserves of scepticism. Sometimes unemotional and pragmatic, sometimes romantic and playful, success-orientated, keen on experimenting and powerful consumers, highly-informed and critical, flexible, and — with regard to the demands of the job market — highly mobile. The individual episodes of the series are not elements of a never-ending set of stories, but focus their attention on one subject, ie. one main plot/problem. Each episode is converted into a self-contained story through one or several narrative story-lines. Subordinate story-lines may be continued, be picked up again and overlap into later episodes in which they become a central theme.

Current situation

The team presented the series to a broadcaster after the first workshop, so did not attend the second.

EVERYTHING WILL BE ALRIGHT: RHEINGOLD-LIMOUSINEN

Peter Paulich, Gerhard Schmidt, Dorothea Neukirchen,
Sytze van der Laan
Gemini Filmproduktion
Mehlemerstrasse 6, 5000 Koln 51, Germany
Tel: 49 221 372046 Fax: 49 221 342571
240 x 25'
Drama serial/comedy

Synopsis

The story is set in a large town in Germany and focusses on Hanna Landwehr's central office for rental cars with drivers. Sitting on a chair in front of a microphone, she directs her assorted group of drivers, one of whom drives the luxury 'stretch' limousine, "the Rheingold". For Hanna, this office is a window on the world, as she experiences amusing, sad, mad, frightening and exciting events. The passengers reflect the troubles, worries, and joys of the people in the town, from the more modest passengers to famous stars and politicians. Some of the stories also involve a small gas station at an intersection in the suburbs, where repairs are done, and a kiosk, about to be turned into a snackbar.

Current situation

During the workshops, the team rewrote one episode and wrote a second, introducing important changes in the tone (more humour), and in the protagonist's character. Subsequently, a new writer was engaged to polish the two episodes and all 10 storylines, after which she, the producers and the script-editor spent two weeks concentrating on finalizing the details of the new concept. The project now awaits the first reactions of a major German public broadcaster.

JUST IN TIME

Albert Vinyoli, Francesc Orteu, Joan Sol
Cromosoma-Imatco
Berlinès 34, 08022 Barcelona, Spain
Tel: 34 3 266 4266 Fax: 34 3 266 3834
26 x 26'
Sitcom\comedy

Synopsis

The owners of a famous brand of Catalan 'cava' face bankruptcy unless they can find partners. They sell 49% of the business to a Japanese multi-national, which sends an executive to supervise the enterprise. The executive's mission is to apply the "Just in Time" production principles, a method developed by Toyota in the '50s, based on reducing production cycles and minimizing stocks. Application of Japanese productions methods and philosophy to the traditional rural Mediterranean world creates all sorts of cultural, personal and family friction, within both the married and business life of the Catalan owners. In the clash between East and West, the Japanese executive starts to discover the pleasures of the good life, while his Catalan counterpart becomes obsessed with the working asceticism of the Japanese. The former's wife is the focus of harmony and discord between the two men.

Current situation

The provisional title during PILOTS referred to a specific production process but the writing carried out by the team led to a broader attitude, of East-meets-West, within the framework of the 'cava' business. Therefore, a new, definitive title was decided: "**From Sun to Sun**", sub-titled "**From the Rising to the Burning Sun**". Apart from re-titling, updating the 'bible' (introducing new characters and eliminating old ones, revising sets, restructuring episodes, etc) negotiations with RTVE continued, and are in their final stages, with good possibilities of an agreement in 1994. The team now has a final version of the first episode, two further episodes requiring some polishing, and treatments for three more episodes.

213

SEXE DÈBIL (THE WEAKER SEX)

Montse Abad, Cuca Canals, Paco Mir, Pepo Sol
Ovideo TV
Sant Eudald 11, Torre, 08023 Barcelona, Spain
Tel: 34 3 219 5162 Fax: 34 3 213 7007
26 x 25'
Sitcom/comedy

Synopsis

This situation comedy portrays the day-to-day life, normal habits and humdrum problems of an average family. However, this apparent normality is not normal at all, because the protagonists do not occupy the traditional roles of 'man the breadwinner' and 'woman the domestic carer'. Quite the opposite. By turning the world upside down in this way, we can see through the absurdity of many social customs and behaviour patterns, especially if we consider that we are on the verge of entering the 21st century. The change of roles provides a vein of humour to be tapped constantly; on the other hand, it also allows us to remain ironic and critical throughout the series. The series is centred on one character immersed in a life-crisis at fifty, who undergoes an evolution towards a liberation that children and spouse take upon themselves to torpedo — a liberation which the character does not at heart really desire that much.

Current situation

As a result of input from experts during the first workshop, the original script and bible was taken to pieces and work started again almost from scratch. Since then, the team has worked continually until feeling confident enough to present it to broadcasters. They are currently awaiting reactions.

GREEK IDYLL

Saskia Sutton, Gordon Render
Blossom Productions
Suite 10, 91 St Martins Lane, London WC2N 0DL, UK
Tel: 44 71 497 3740 Fax: 44 71 497 3740
7 x 60'
Comedy/drama series

Synopsis

Mickey, Herbie and Amethyst are all on the run. From thugs, money problems and life... Due to circumstances that are entirely their fault, they find themselves stuck together on a tatty, wooden, ocean-going ketch berthed in a marina on one of the Greek Isles. With cash-flow problems and the boat as their only asset, they form a 'plan' — that is, to make a lucrative living chartering the boat to tourists along the Mediterranean coast. The problem is, none of them has ever done it before and, combined with a disastrous series of tourists, their enterprise could be best described as "the boat-charter from Hell".

Current situation

With substantial re-writing between the two workshops, the project now has a fully-developed package: character studies of the main parts, script, outlines for all 7 episodes and two well-known actors attached. The producer has sent the material to several interested European broadcasters for possible co-production. In the UK, ITV and the BBC are both considering the project.

THE IMAGEMAKERS

Peter Gren Larsen, Poul Erik Carstensen, Svend Abrahamsen
Danmarks Radio-TV, 2860 Soeborg, Denmark
Tel: 45 35 203040 Fax: 45 35 204200
6 x 25'
Sitcom/Comedy

Synopsis

From the dawn of time, man has been searching desperately for an identity. These days, this desperate search has been turned into a very profitable business by people in advertising. But lurking behind the slick façade of fast cars and designer-jeans, lie the doubts and uncertainties of these same people. Should morals be sacrificed in the attempt to gain clients? How long can one survive if betraying one's own principles on a daily basis? These conflicts, and others, within the business itself provide us with the perfect basis for a very human and very entertaining look into the perhaps not so wonderful world of advertising.

Current situation

After the second workshop, the script of the first episode was commissioned, but the project was eventually cancelled by Danmarks Radio, with permission for the writers to seek other backers, which they are currently doing.

CREDITS

GENERAL COUNCIL

Media Business School, Generalitat de Catalunya, Televisió de Catalunya

EXECUTIVE COMMITTEE

Fernando Labrada (MBS), Antonio Saura (MBS),
Antoni Kirchner (Generalitat de Catalunya), Oleguer Sarsanedas (TVC)

ORGANISATION

Pere Roca	*Managing Director*
Julian Friedmann	*Head of Studies*
Thomas Spieker	*Administrator*
Jane Busfield and Judi Sydes	*Assistants*

ADVISORY COUNCIL

Peter Ansorge (Channel 4), Siegfried Braun (ZDF), Poul Malmkjaer (DR),
Renee Goddard / Christian Routh (ESF), Roberto Pace (RAI),
Antonio Saura (MBS), Julian Friedmann (PILOTS), Pere Roca (PILOTS)

EXPERTS 1993

Tutors

Doc Comparato, Adrian Hodges, Pascal Lonhay, Guy Meredith, Jürgen Wolff

Godparents

Karin Bamborough (NRK), Siegfried Braun (ZDF), Clive Brill (BBC),
Paul Malmkjaer (Danmarks Radio), Roberto Pace (RAI)

Specialists

Jason Brett (TriStar Television), Jean Pierre Dusseaux (Communauté des
Télévisions Francophones), Lilie Ferrari ("**EastEnders**"), Rift Fournier ("**Kojak**"),
Jeanne Glynn ("**General Hospital**"), Corinne Hollingworth ("**EastEnders**"),
Jeffrey Lewis ("**Hill Street Blues**"), Caryn Mandabach ("**The Cosby Show**",
"**Roseanne**"), Stephan Warnik (RTL), Humphrey Barclay ("**Desmond's**"),
Renée Goddard (European Script Fund), Fernando Labrada (Media Business
School), Gudie Lawaetz (Television Business School), Linda Seger (script analyst),
Paulette Randall ("**Desmond's**"), Renate Roginas (Telfrance),
Christian Routh (European Script Fund), Greg Snow ("**Casualty**"),
John Wells ("**China Beach**")

Broadcasters

Peter Ansorge (Channel 4), Anat Birnbaum (Canal Plus), Matthias Esche (NDR),
Ronald Gräbe (WDR), Margaret Nicoll (Canal Plus), Wim Odé (NOS),
Nicolas Saada (ARTE), Miguel Salvat (Canal Plus), Oleguer Sarsanedas (TV3),
Monika Schmid (SDR)

STAFF DURING THE WORKSHOPS 1993

Heather Wylie	*Marical & Technical Co-Ordinator*
Inés Roca	*Hotel & Hospitality Co-Ordinator*
Lourdes Vidal-Ribas	*Travel Co-Ordinator*
Gemma Delgado	*Runner*
Michael Aloy	*Runner*
Albert Royo	*Technician*
Oriol Subirana	*Technician*
Jordi Casas	*Technician*
Gemma Marsa	*Hostess*
Sabina Jessen	*Hostess*

EXPERTS WHO PARTICIPATED IN PILOTS FEASIBILITY STUDY 1992

Keith Aberdein, Lone Bastholm, Lynn Bayonas, Sigvard Bennetzen, Leo Benvenuti, Rainer Berg, Michel Bergmann, Bruce Best, David Blake-Knox, Emilio Bolles, Conny Brak, Siegfried Braun, Bob Bremer, Jason Brett, Martha Burke Hennessy, Wesley Burrowes, Jaume Cabré, Isabel Chaves, Bo Christensen, Doc Comparato, Dennis Cooper, Philippe Cottereau, Gaspard de Chavagnac, Michalis Dimitriou, Daphne Djaferi, Alain Donzel, Jorge Duarte, Paul Duggan, Esteve Duran, Charles Elton, Wolfgang Esterer, Tony Fahy, Jan Fantl, Frank Feiter, Lluís Ferrando, Lilie Ferrari, Kenneth Fitts, Rift Fournier, Dirk Frisch, Tom Gabbay, Hans Galesloot, David García, Jeanne Glynn, Renee Goddard, Giancarlo Guastini, Chris Gunn, Patrick Harbinson, Dana Hastier, Susi Hush, Age Incrocci, Henrik Iversen, Carles Jover, V. Katsanis, Paul Kieffer, Mogens Klovedal, Lakis Kominos, Jutta Lieck, Ingrad Luker, Brendon Lunney, Kevin Malloy, Poul Malmkjaer, Caryn Mandabach, Marie Françoise Mascaro, Marie Masmonteil, Robert McKee, Guy Meredith, Greg Millin, Isy Morgensztern, Tony Morphett, Robert Nador, Kaj Nissen, Ricardo Nogueira, Lise Norgaard, Steven North, Joaquín Oristrell, Andries Overste, T. Papathanassiou, David Paulsen, Jobst Plog, Dimitrios Pontikas, Beth Porter, Mark Princi, José María Quintana, Elvira Ralli, Isabel Raventós, Tom Reeve, Gary Reilly, Chantal Remy, M. Reppas, Keith Richardson, Gerd Richter-Kiewning, Mercedes Rico, Lucía Rikaki, Cecile Roger-Marchant, Colin Rogers, Jean Rouilly, Christian Routh, Jacques Rouzet, Paul Rozenberg, Lola Salvador, Claude Santelli, Oleguer Sarsanedas, Romain Schroeder, Michael Smeaton, Anton Smit, Ben Stassen, Peter Sterz, Jovanna Tembou, Paul Thitges, Ricardo Tozzi, Marja Tutert, Dagmar Ungureit, Edwin van Meurs, Vassilis Vassilikos, Stephan Warnik, Steve Wasserman, Eileen Wasserman, Christian Watton, Linda Wendell, Thomas Wesskamp, Tim Whitby, Dick Willemsen, Moira Williams, Katrina Wood, Beth Worth, Michael Zagor, Achim Zons